THE ANXIOUS
PERSONALITY

THE ANXIOUS PERSONALITY

Dissolving the Hidden Components of Anxiety

Timothy Lin

Founder of The Anxious Personality Framework

STAR HOUSE PUBLISHING

Carmel Valley, CA

2023

DISCLAIMER

The author makes no guarantees that readers will achieve specific results by reading this book. All personal development is unique to the individual. The results and client case studies presented in this book represent results achieved working directly with the author. Your results may vary when undertaking your own inner work.

Star House Publishing

Printed in the United States of America

31640 Via la Estrella
Carmel Valley, CA 93924

ISBN: 979-8-9874137-1-5

First Printing Edition, 2023

Dedicated to the boldness, love,
and unwavering compassion
of Presence.

CONTENTS

INTRODUCTION

T his book exists because I know first-hand how difficult it is to do anything with anxiety. When you have anxiety—especially anxiety that's embedded into your personality structure—it's so easy to think that you're just an anxious person and it's something you'll always have.

So limiting yourself becomes a normal thing to do—you stop going for the promotion, you stop yourself from pursuing projects that put you in the spotlight, and you don't allow yourself to follow your natural impulse to do things you're passionate about because the anxiety has too strong of a grip, whether it's overt or quietly hiding beneath the surface.

Or maybe you're able to do all these things and do them well, but you find yourself continually fighting against a nagging, persistent kind of anxiety. Others may see you as put-together and competent, but your own inner experience is completely different, and you feel as if you have to put on a mask for the world. But most of all, anxiety keeps you from being present in your life. Before I systematically worked through my own anxiety, I missed many, many moments and many, many opportunities. Today, I get to enjoy the sweetness and delight of my work, my family, and those around me.

Obviously, "anxiety-free" means different things to different people. For the purposes of this book, living your life without anxiety, or at least significantly less anxiety, is a huge win. What I've found for myself and for my clients is that if you follow the framework in this book, anxiety begins to dissolve and melt away until we're completely free of it. We can be unburdened, simple, and relaxed.

In my experience, that's what true confidence is. It's not brazen, showy, or even necessarily bold. Instead, it's deeply being with ourselves, no matter where we are or what we're experiencing. This could mean a variety of things. It could mean that you level up at work. It could mean that you start a new relationship without so much insecurity. Or it could mean that you can set boundaries with more clarity and decisiveness. The list goes on and on. All these things are easier without anxiety, and for me, life without anxiety intrinsically means peace, confidence, trust, and success.

To help you achieve that, this book will take you through **The Anxious Personality Framework**, a system that I've created over the last two decades to understand the hidden components that create anxiety and how to dissolve them. In Part 1, I'll outline the Anxious Personality, which is the central operating system that creates and maintains the anxiety that you've likely identified with for most of your life. We'll examine the most common anxiety patterns, how to recognize them, and ultimately how to dismantle them to reconnect with your essential confidence.

In Part 2, you'll learn how to use the **Direct Inquiry Method**, a technique that I learned and distilled across a variety of therapies and spiritual approaches. This is where we'll deep dive into each of the components of the Anxious Personality, so you understand exactly where your anxiety comes from, why it's there, and why it has stayed for so long.

Part 3 is workbook-based and where the work happens. It contains the Direct Inquiry prompts and exercises that I take my one-on-one coaching clients through. In this section, you'll be able to explore how the components of the Anxious Personality impact you specifically and start to realize what being anxiety-free can be like.

By the end of the book, you'll have at minimum loosened your identification with the Anxious Personality and experienced your initial glimpses of having enough emotional and mental space to just be yourself. My hope is that you'll know that the Anxious Personality is not who you are and that you can live your life without anxiety.

As optimistic a vision as this might seem, what I want the most is for you to take back the essential power that you've disowned and experience real healing. While this might sound daunting, it only means learning how to simply be yourself and trusting that being you is enough. The entirety of this book can be summarized like this:

- **Point #1:** The Anxious Personality is an operating system containing the source code that runs the program of anxiety.

- **Point #2:** To free yourself from that programming, you need to understand the underlying components of that code, why it's there, and how to dissolve it.

- **Point #3:** To become anxiety-free, you don't need new programming by creating a "new you" or messing with the subconscious. You simply need to reconnect with your natural sense of confidence, power, and security.

The biggest result of using The Anxious Personality Framework is that you'll be able to live your life in a more dynamic, fulfilled, and purposeful way. When you don't have anxiety holding you back, you live free. You free your heart. You free your mind and open to what's possible. You free your creativity. And, whatever concepts you might have of it, you free your soul.

I've created this framework so you don't have to spend the two decades of personal, psychological, and spiritual development that I spent figuring out what works. Hopefully, you can start embodying an anxiety-free life much sooner than I did. My life's work is about helping you understand your anxiety so you can not only be free from how painful it is but also for you to be authentically yourself. I hope that this book contributes to relieving your anxiety and the collective anxiety of our times.

PART ONE

THE PROBLEM OF ANXIETY

CHAPTER 1

THE ANXIOUS
PERSONALITY

I was severely depressed with a high degree of anxiety about work and adulting when I began my journey toward healing anxiety. I had dealt with anxiety and depression since I was 16, and it wasn't until I was 26 that I started to become aware of the negative thoughts that constantly ran underneath the surface of my consciousness.

What I discovered was that a large part of my anxiety and insecurity had to do with a critical inner voice, which is widely referred to as the Inner Critic. I came to see how automatically I took those messages to be true. When I started to create more distance from the Inner Critic, I began to see that this voice was the very thing that was making me feel down and out.

I used to describe it as a one-two punch. The Inner Critic would push me to do something it deemed productive (left jab). I would go do it, and it would criticize me about how I did it or that it wasn't up to the high standard that it was setting for me (right hook). Or I would fail to do something, and it would say, "Oh, you didn't do that, you're so undisciplined, how are you going to be successful? (uppercut)." These inner exchanges would inevitably leave me KO'd, and it took me a long time to realize this inner voice was making everything really difficult.

It wasn't as if things were terrible. I had a job as a freelance editor and writer, I was supporting myself, I had friends that I went out with regularly...but the anxiety I experienced day in and day out was exhausting. It always felt like I had some gravitational pull inside that would suck me in and fill me with dread.

During my first year of wrestling with the Inner Critic, I would get knocked down frequently without even knowing why. Sometimes, I'd be able to look back and realize, "Oh, I feel scared about doing this project because the Inner Critic is telling me I'm going to completely humiliate myself." After a few months, I started to get better at catching the Inner Critic in the act, and I could start to challenge it. Most of the time, I'd get overpowered by its authoritative claims that I wasn't good enough or I had done this or that thing wrong. But sometimes, I could see through the Inner Critic enough that it wouldn't debilitate me because I had (sort of) stopped believing it.

At the same time, I got into approaches like the Law of Attraction, and I went deep into positive affirmations, trying to plant enough thoughts about being confident that it would change all the subconscious thinking about how I couldn't be confident or successful (you'll learn why that doesn't work long-term in Chapter 4). And even though I was taking anti-depressants and anti-anxiety medication, I felt as if I was disconnected from myself. The medications helped me manage my anxiety but didn't resolve the anxiety itself. The anxiety would always come back, and sometimes even more severely than before. I thought I had successfully "beaten" anxiety, but I found myself experiencing the same tension, the same nervousness, and the same near-panic triggers that I had before. I spent the next ten years figuring out why.

THE TURNING POINT

I was fortunate enough to stumble upon different trainings, roughly in the same span of five to ten years, which would eventually be the building blocks for The Anxious Personality Framework. The first was Nonviolent Communication, a framework created by Marshal Rosenberg that's centered on non-judgment and the concept that judgment stems from tragically unmet needs. The training I received in Nonviolent Communication showed me that the feeling of anxiety could be tied to a deeply unmet need for something universal and essential in us.

The second was the Enneagram system, which has become mainstream in popular culture, especially in leadership development circles. But it was the teachings of Russ Hudson and Sandra Maitri, pioneers within the Enneagram space, that helped me to understand the distinction between the "fixed, limited personality" and "our true nature."

The third was The Diamond Approach, a modern spiritual approach that combined psychological and spiritual understanding to realize our true nature. A.H. Almaas, the founder of The Diamond Approach, put forward the "theory of holes" in his teaching, which is a major foundational principle for The Anxious Personality Framework. In short, the theory of holes states that the ego personality develops from a disconnection from an essential part of our true selves, and this disconnection is the primary source of our suffering, which can take the form of anger, despair, envy, hatred, fear, and of course, anxiety.

As a student of The Diamond Approach, I learned a great deal about ego development and what makes up the "ego structure," or what is widely known as the fixed personality. The personality is how we generally know ourselves. It's what gives you a sense of self, a sense of "you" versus "me." While most of us walk around assuming we are the personality, I discovered through my training that the personality is not much more than the sum of the programming and conditioning that we've internalized in our life.

Understanding this became the secret key to understanding why despite years of meditation, cognitive behavior therapy, counseling, prayer, positive affirmations, and law of attraction work, I still hadn't overcome this nagging, sometimes debilitating anxiety. Or why I'd feel better in meditation but the minute I had to ask my boss for time off or share my opinion in a meeting, anxiety would get triggered and I'd feel small, incapable, and sometimes downright terrified.

I discovered that the anxiety itself was embedded in my personality. Without understanding and dismantling my identification with the personality, everything I tried was only temporary relief. In psychological terms, this kind of anxiety is called "trait anxiety." The American Psychological Association defines as "a proneness to experience anxiety." In other words, this kind of anxiety is part of the personality and isn't only experienced in certain situations that are inherently more stressful, such as an interview setting or a high-stakes presentation. That kind of situational anxiety is called "state anxiety."

Despite years of studying the ego/personality, I had yet to come across any approach that specifically dealt with an anxious personality type, but with my clients, I came to see that there was a specific type of personality structure that oriented itself around anxiety. This is what I eventually called the "Anxious Personality." Based on my training in the Enneagram and ego development, I realized that there are specific components that make up this kind of personality, and that it had common effects on people who experienced the same kind of chronic trait anxiety that I did.

It turns out that the Inner Critic is only one component of the personality, and even though it's the gateway to understand and dismantle the Anxious Personality, there are three other components to disengage from to be able to dissolve anxiety completely. Together, they act as a kind of system that continually outputs anxiety.

We'll cover the components and how to dismantle them in detail in Part 2, but I want to at least introduce a summary of each component and generally how they create anxiety in the Anxious Personality.

- **The Inner Critic:** This is part of our psyche that dictates what is acceptable or not acceptable in our experience. It watches and polices our behavior. It judges who we are and tells us how we should be, so it causes a great deal of the anxiety we experience in our daily lives.

  To dismantle this part of the Anxious Personality, you need to be able to recognize what an Inner Critic Message feels like, identify where it came from, and learn how to effectively disengage from it. Most people, even if they've recognized self-criticism and worked with it to some extent, are still functioning by unconsciously following the Inner Critic's orders because they underestimate how pervasive it is in the Anxious Personality. I'll detail how this works in Chapter 6.

- **The Sense of Self:** This is how you tend to think of yourself or how you know yourself to be "you." People who struggle with anxiety are often tightly identified with an identity that is weak, overwhelmed, or unimportant. In Chapter 7, we'll explore how this identity actually forms and how to reorient to a more authentic Sense of Self.

- **The Core Belief:** This is the core component that runs all the programming of the Anxious Personality. It's a generally mistaken belief that the entire personality structure builds its worldview around. Largely unconscious, this belief was likely formed in early childhood, so it typically goes unchallenged or feels like it's even beyond questioning.

  We'll examine the concept of the core belief in Chapter 8 and why we continue to support our anxious worldview and disregard any evidence that challenges our anxiety.

- **The Anxiety Template:** This is the basic template that codes how the Anxious Personality should relate to others. You'll see that we tend to unconsciously overlay this Anxiety Template onto others. For the Anxious Personality, the Anxiety Template generally dictates something along the lines of, "I should be small and the other person has all the power." We'll learn more about how this happens, how to recognize when you're doing it, and how to stop it from happening in Chapter 9.

As I learned more about these components and worked with my own Anxious Personality, I began to experience longer and longer periods of time without anxiety, as if I were free from it altogether, until the Anxious Personality was no longer in the driver's seat at all. This has been life-changing, to say the least. It's one thing to try to convince yourself that you don't need to be anxious. It's an entirely different thing to directly know to the core of your being that you are safe, secure, accepted, and perfectly okay just as you are.

If I had to summarize the benefits I've experienced because of this approach to anxiety, I would point to a number of different outcomes:

Anxiety-Free Functioning

Today, I'm able to move through my life and work with significantly less anxiety. There are still times when the Anxious Personality will pop up here or there if I'm in a particularly triggering situation, but my general baseline is a quiet mind and a relaxed body. And in those ultra-challenging moments, I can quickly go through the four components of the Anxious Personality and free myself from their grip.

I often describe this work as the equivalent to going to the gym. On its own, going to the gym isn't really going to help you in an actionable way in the moment. It's only when you have to help move a heavy couch or pick up your toddler over and over again that having done your workout is helpful. It gives you the capacity to function in a particular way. The same thing holds true with anxiety-free functioning. Doing the work to understand the Anxious Personality gives you the capacity to freely function with security and confidence.

When the Anxious Personality isn't in the driver's seat, living your daily life simply becomes easier and more doable, no matter what situation or context you're in. As a specific example, we recently had a lot of rain and flooding in the area where I live and as a result, we had a landslide in the back of our house. One of our drainage pipes had broken and a lot of water then collected and allowed the hillside to slide. Before having "worked out" the Anxious Personality Framework, I would likely have let the Anxious Personality criticize me for not knowing to maintain the drainage pipes, and then it would have criticized me while I tried to take care of the issue. And all of that would have made me sluggish, deflated, unmotivated, and overwhelmed. Instead, I was able to simply focus on one step at a time, one problem at a time, and one solution at a time—all the while being in contact with my own competence, skill, intelligence, and capacity.

Most people who tell me that the Anxious Personality Framework resonates with them are actually people who are successful in their lives. Success and anxiety aren't mutually exclusive. But succeeding with anxiety is not only harder, it's also not very enjoyable. I've found that success without anxiety is possible, and I assure you it's the preferable option!

Anxiety-Free Relationships

From a social perspective, this work results in more ease and less anxiety meeting new people and developing meaningful connections. Prior to dismantling the Anxious Personality, I was anxious and withdrawn at social functions at work, going out to dinner with clients, or even attending parties for my kids. I felt unable to come out of my shell, and in most cases, anxiety would feel too large for me to overcome.

Nowadays, I don't feel the need to hide or withdraw anymore. This gives me much more freedom to have real connection with others, especially the new people in my life. It's allowed me to build more authentic connections. It's as if I can miraculously be myself while also allowing others to be themselves because I no longer operate from the Anxious Personality. I'm still introverted. I still prefer quiet time and contemplating things on my own, but my preference for solitude is no longer driven by a debilitating sense of anxiety or feeling not enough.

Meaningful Work

Most importantly, being able to pursue work that has meaning and purpose is the most impactful outcome of this framework. Freeing myself from the Anxious Personality has allowed me to pursue my passion for coaching, transformation, and helping others overcome anxiety. When the Anxious Personality is running the show, it becomes really hard to align to how your authentic nature would naturally want to express itself. The Anxious Personality is like a big dam that has blocked up all this potential, and when you dismantle the dam, the water is allowed to freely flow again. In my case, the Anxious Personality kept me operating within its programming, which constricted what I could do for work. *You have to have a stable salary. You need to do something respectful.*

You need to keep striving for promotions or else you aren't growing. You need to keep up! Forget your passion, it's more important to be practical. Freeing myself from this messaging brought me back into contact with an inner strength, confidence, and knowing that helping others is the most natural expression of my own being and what I am most suited to do. With that, I'm able to pursue work that has meaning and purpose.

Your Intrinsic Value

This one isn't really a measurable outcome, but a direct result of dismantling the Anxious Personality is directly knowing your intrinsic value. The Anxious Personality constantly creates this pressure to be somebody that you're supposed to be. It creates a pressure to follow the rules and the conditioning that's programmed for us. In other words, it prevents us from being in contact with who you really are—that is, someone with value, regardless of what you do or how you do it. Just *being yourself* is valuable because by nature, *you are valuable.* It's easy to understand this mentally. It's another thing to know it through and through. So I find it immensely valuable to directly know myself, to be in touch with my own experience, and therefore feel the inherent support of love, safety, security, confidence, and capacity. What can't you do with all that under your belt?

CASE STUDIES

Because this approach to understanding and dismantling the Anxious Personality is systematized, it means that it has the same results for those who go through it. Here are a few case studies of clients who have worked with me to dissolve the Anxious Personality:

Grace

Grace reached out to me like many of my clients who struggle with anxiety and overwhelm. In her own words, she wrote, "I seem to experience myself as depressed and anxious and frustrated and stressed and on edge all the time." By using the Direct Inquiry Method (covered in Chapter 5), we identified a host of Inner Critic judgments that were making Grace feel depressed, heavy, and anxious. This was the first major breakthrough because the Inner Critic was *causing* her anxiety so consistently that she was completely identified with that experience.

It took her some time to shift from saying "I'm beating myself up for being lazy and not taking care of my health" to recognizing that the Inner Critic was saying, *"You're* not taking care of your health and because of that, you're lazy!" Once she started using the technique to disarm the Inner Critic that you'll learn in Chapter 6, she was able to feel free and spacious again and experience what it was like to not have the Inner Critic constantly badgering her.

Having this inner space freed Grace up to explore her Sense of Self. She saw that she always thought of herself as easygoing but also quite powerless, and she traced this anxiety back to her relationship with her mother, whom she experienced as hypercritical growing up. She loved her mother and could see her mother's compassion, but she was also acutely aware of her mother's judgments and how they affected her daily life. When she explored this further using the Direct Inquiry Method, she got in touch with the deep hurt her mother's judgments had left on her and the Core Belief that she wasn't good enough.

Through one-on-one coaching, Grace also was able to see how her relationship with her mother had become a core part of her Anxiety Template, and how she tended to always play the role of the small, overwhelmed child while other people in her life had all the power. As Grace went through the steps to understand and dismantle the Anxious Personality, she came to see how tightly the Anxious Personality had her bound up. After each step, she became freer and freer:

> *"I've been working with Timothy for just 3 weeks now. And I struggle to put into words how life giving, lifesaving, and life affirming this work and these sessions have been. I feel relief. I have been able to let go of a dark cloud that was hanging around me for years. There is no striving to be a 'certain way' to gain approval. After a little hesitation, I'm beginning to feel and see and know that I am fully accepted to be where I am and to be with that and move from there."*

After our time together, Grace went on to get married, transition into a new career, and even saw marked improvement in her relationship with her mother. If you're like Grace and find yourself up against a lot of self-criticism from one of your core relationships, Chapter 6 will be particularly helpful as I lay out how to identify, understand, and disarm the Inner Critic.

Jamie

Jamie contacted me because she was pursuing a music career that was continually putting her outside her comfort zone. She was experiencing a lot of anxiety and fear, and generally felt burdened by self-criticism and expectations. We quickly got to see that her Inner Critic would consistently tell her that she wasn't doing things well enough. Not only that, but it would also judge her for not doing enough things *and* also for not being able to complete anything. After clearly seeing how her Inner Critic was creating a lose-lose situation, she started to get better at disarming the Inner Critic.

However, when she would get in front of the mic or begin recording, the anxiety would pop up again and she wouldn't know why. As we continued through the Anxious Personality Framework, she began to see that the Sense of Self was constricted to the "perfect one," where everything about her had to be perfect or she would get criticized, judged or humiliated. As she explored this further, she got more in touch with her Anxiety Template, and saw that as a child, her mother would constantly set her up to fail and want her to do better.

She saw how she was projecting this template onto others, thinking that others were expecting her to be perfect when that actually wasn't the case. For Jamie, her Core Belief had to do with not being valued for who she was, and she saw that she always had to be doing something to gain approval from her mother. This led her to see that her anxiety was always about needing to feel valued, and if she didn't do something well enough, she would feel the horrible humiliation that she experienced as a child.

As she saw how the Anxious Personality was responsible for making her feel overwhelmed and insecure, she saw how she was constantly running her experiences of pursuing her music, parenting her two kids, and tackling other projects through her Anxious Personality. In her own words:

> *"This has taken my self-awareness to the next level by allowing me to gain perspective about the Anxious Personality. It has helped me get to the root of what keeps me playing small and as a result I have learned to give myself permission to release my stuck, negative emotions and move on to a more promising present and future, without the defeating voices keeping me pinned to the past."*

Jamie's Anxious Personality created a dynamic that made her feel overwhelmed by super high standards, so her anxiety was about never being able to do things "right." If you experience a similar dynamic, deep diving into the anxiety pattern of perfectionism, covered in Chapter 3, will be really important to understand how components of the Anxious Personality create and maintain a need to be "the best."

Eric

Eric was a 30-year-old professional who had been feeling "directionally lost" in his career. On our discovery call, he shared how he had been feeling overwhelmed by the pandemic and his mental health was suffering from repeated burnout and stress. He wanted to "break the cycle" and find a better way to show up, both personally and professionally.

Eric was quick to understand the basic components of the Anxious Personality. He found that his Inner Critic would constantly push him to not feel his emotions and put on a happy face or to push through his feelings by working harder. He was surprised to see that a lot of the personal development work he'd done played into the Inner Critic's programming of "being positive."

As Eric learned how to disarm the Inner Critic, he came to see how the Inner Critic pushed him to always be "not a bother." If he could be reliable to others or not be a burden, he would be able to relax. But that never ended up happening for long. Because his Sense of Self had an identity of being lackluster and middle of the road, any time he felt like he could be more expansive, he would experience anxiety.

Eric's Anxiety Template was extremely clear: He was not to rock the boat, and the other people in his life were too busy for him. When he saw this, he also came into direct contact with the mistaken Core Belief that he didn't matter. This belief ended up creating anxiety a lot at work because his role required him to "be seen." So when the attention was on him, the anxiety would amplify.

As Eric completed each stage of this framework, he became more aware of the patterns of the Anxious Personality and how they made him feel. As he learned to disengage with them, he also became more confident and secure in his decision-making and more comfortable being in the limelight. After our work together, Eric wrote:

> *"The impact I've experienced after only 3 months has been life changing! From working through Inner Critic messaging to unlocking and acknowledging past trauma, understanding the Anxious Personality has helped guide me on a path to rebuilding self-trust and regaining internal balance.*
>
> *Not only do I feel equipped with tools for breaking down the Anxious Personality, but I also feel a renewed sense of self-confidence and groundedness. Timothy's approach is empathetic, constructive, and results-focused, and I am excited to continue the next phase of my coaching journey with him!*

Shortly after going through the initial stages of the program, Eric resigned from a position that he was unhappy with and switched to a role that was more aligned with his values and interests. He also reported that in his friendships and work relationships, he felt more confident and able to set appropriate boundaries, something that he felt too anxious to do before.

BECOMING ANXIETY-FREE

As you can see, every person has different aspects of the Anxious Personality that affect them in different ways, and being able to dismantle it empowers them to do different things in their lives. In Chapter 3, you'll learn about the primary anxiety patterns of the Anxious Personality and how they create different "flavors" of anxiety that impact your life. We'll also go through each of the steps that the clients above went through in detail in Part 2, but for now, consider: Each of these clients are experiencing a version of an anxiety-free life after learning how to disengage from the Anxious Personality.

They no longer have to deal with anxiety on a day-to-day, moment-to-moment basis. They no longer have to over-prepare and overwork. They no longer have to be "perfect." What they do in their lives and at work has become exponentially easier because they aren't hypervigilant about how they need to be. They are no longer spending time worrying, doubting themselves, or figuring out ways to "stay safe." Instead, they are simply able to stay more present, which means they are able to show up more fully in their endeavors in their personal and professional lives.

For some, this means they are more easily able to pursue work that is more aligned and more life-giving. For others, it means they are pursuing life goals that scared them too much before, like adopting a child or moving to a new state. But most importantly, they can enjoy the pleasure, peacefulness, and love in their lives because the Anxious Personality is no longer in the way. That is the goal of this approach. My hope is that you'll experience this freedom and show up fully in your life and work, because I know that when you do, the world will become a better place and those in your life will benefit in ways you can't even imagine yet.

SELF-ASSESSMENT

The purpose of this self-assessment is to discern whether you are experiencing "state anxiety" or "trait anxiety." High scores in trait anxiety indicate that anxiety is part of the personality, which is specifically what the Anxious Personality Framework is designed to address.[1]

Question Set 1

Read each statement as a description of how you feel **right now, in this moment.** Don't think too much about any one question but just respond based on what seems to describe your present feelings the best.

	Not at all	Some -what	Moder -ately so	Very much so
I feel upset.	1	2	3	4
I feel frightened.	1	2	3	4
I feel nervous.	1	2	3	4
I feel jittery.	1	2	3	4
I feel confused.	1	2	3	4

Tally up your score here: ___13___

---

[1] Note: This assessment is adapted from the Spielberger State-Trait Anxiety Inventory (STAI) for Adults, developed by Charles D. Spielberger. This shorter version was created by Andras N. Zsido et. al.

Question Set 2

For this next set of statements, circle the number at the end of the statement that best indicates how you **generally feel**.

	Not at all	Some -what	Moder -ately so	Very much so
I feel that difficulties are piling up so that I can't overcome them.	1	2	3	4
I worry too much over things that doesn't really matter.	1	2	3	4
Unimportant thoughts run through my mind and bother me.	1	2	3	4
I take disappointments so hard that I can't put them out of my mind.	1	2	3	4
I get in a state of tension or turmoil as I think over my recent concerns and interests.	1	2	3	4

Tally up your score here: ___15___

How to Interpret Your Scores

The score to Question Set 1 is your "state anxiety score."

- *Greater or equal than 15:* There are likely multiple stressors in your life causing you high anxiety. Creating time and space to distance yourself from these stressors by practicing meditation, yoga, breathwork, etc. will help. In conjunction, you may want to find a professional mental health specialist for additional support.

- *Between 7 and 14:* You may have a specific situation you are dealing with that is causing moderate anxiety. You can use basic coping strategies to help alleviate the anxiety, but likely it will subside once the situation is resolved.

- *Less than 6:* Anxiety is likely not an issue for you at this moment, but the contents in this book will help you to understand how personality structures are formed and also help you to better understand or support someone in your life who struggles with anxiety.

The score to Question Set 2 is your "trait anxiety score."

- *Greater than or equal to 15:* This indicates that you have a high degree of trait anxiety and likely have anxiety embedded into your personality. This book and its concepts will help you understand where this anxiety likely came from. In addition, you may also want to get the support of a professional health specialist while working through the exercises in this book.

- *Between 7 and 14:* You likely have components of the Anxious Personality impacting your day-to-day life and limiting your ability to function without anxiety, although you're generally "high functioning." I wrote this book specifically for you!

- *Less than 6:* This is a low "trait anxiety" score, which indicates that while you may experience anxiety from time to time, it's not an integral part of your personality.

KEY CHAPTER TAKEAWAYS

- The Anxious Personality Framework is influenced by a variety of approaches, including Nonviolent Communication (NVC), The Enneagram, and The Diamond Approach.

- A key distinction in the Anxious Personality Framework is the difference between "trait anxiety" and "state anxiety." Trait anxiety is embedded in someone's personality, whereas state anxiety is generally dependent on a specific situation.

- A fundamental principle of the Anxious Personality Framework is that people with "trait anxiety" are prone to experiencing anxiety because of how they responded to a disconnection from a core sense of support, security, value, and confidence.

- The four major components of the Anxious Personality are The Inner Critic, The Sense of Self, The Core Belief, and The Anxiety Template.

- Reconnecting to inner confidence and dissolving anxiety results in anxiety-free functioning, whether it's in your personal life or at work, in social settings or intimate relationships. It's no longer about "getting through anxiety." It's simply about being yourself, which is effortless and relaxed when you've reclaimed your intrinsic value.

CHAPTER 2

WHO THIS BOOK IS FOR

T he framework you are about to learn came from my own struggles with anxiety and trying to "figure it out." Like most people who carry around an Anxious Personality, I felt that anxiety kept me from living optimally at work and in my relationships. Even with my anxiety, I was a high achiever and by cultural standards I was achieving "success." I was rising quickly at a digital marketing agency, getting promoted every two years and getting significant raises. But I continually felt like I was still constantly fighting against anxiety, fear, and self-doubt, no matter how much validation I got from others.

Meditation was a life-changer, but the moment I came out of meditation and opened my computer, the anxiety would immediately blast my system again. I joined a spiritual community to learn how to pray, thinking that surrendering or letting go of my attachments would help, but sure enough, no matter how much I prayed for peace before client meetings, the anxiety would tag along.

Through the years, I did various modes of therapy, including psychotherapy, cognitive behavior therapy, and even psychedelic-assisted therapy. These provided flashes of insight, but anxiety continued to hang around and impact my life. After deep diving into emotional intelligence training, I eventually got certified to teach it. But I found that many of the EQ techniques focused on managing triggers instead of working through the actual cause of these triggers.

At work, I over-prepared, over-worked, and over-thought just about everything. Anxiety would push me toward perfectionistic tendencies to create a feeling of "safety." I would lie awake at night and think about client meetings I had the next day, trying to plan out what I would say and how I was going to say it. After every client meeting or after every new business pitch, I would feel relief, but then the same cycle would start again with the next meeting or the next presentation. As the years went on, the time between cycles got shorter and shorter until burnout was right around the corner.

If any of this resonates with you, then this book is for you. Dismantling the Anxious Personality is most effective for people who:

- Have built enough of a foundation of self-awareness that they can identify inner thoughts and emotions.

- Are functioning well in their lives but are doing so with a degree of anxiety that limits optimal functioning.

- Intuitively feel like there must be a reason for their anxiety and want to understand why.

- Want to invest the time, money, and energy to understand and work through the different components of the Anxious Personality.

The reason why I'm laying out this criteria is because while I hope this book will be helpful to all, I also know from experience that if you have anxiety that is keeping you from holding a job, keeping you completely isolated from friends and family, or is putting you or others in danger, the most effective approach is to see a mental health specialist who can help you with basic coping mechanisms. In addition, while the techniques and concepts of the Anxious Personality Framework will help people who have experienced trauma-induced anxiety, my experience is that trauma-specific approaches are needed to fully resolve trauma and suggest finding a specialist to support your healing in conjunction with this work.

REORIENTING TOWARD SELF-ACCEPTANCE

The #1 mistake that most people who struggle with an Anxious Personality make is trying to get rid of anxiety. You might have picked up this book with the same mentality. For me, I would put on my positive thinking hat and load up on mantras or affirmations, and this gave me a way to be functional at work, but it was always a fight underneath the surface. As one of my clients said about the experience, "You can tell yourself all these things about how you are okay, but anxiety isn't logical. It doesn't listen to your brain."

What this all boils down to is that you need to start with self-acceptance. Whenever I work with my coaching clients, I reorient them toward accepting their anxiety and the feelings that come with that experience. Most clients come to me really wanting to be different, or they've spent a lot of time and energy trying to "fix" themselves because the experience of anxiety is so uncomfortable.

But when it comes to anxiety, trying to make ourselves different or better ends up backfiring on us. It creates even more anxiety because it only adds more fuel to the Anxious Personality. Trying to "fix" anxiety actually makes it worse because the primary cause of anxiety is a disconnection to essential acceptance and value. Like Buckminster Fuller famously said, "You never change things by fighting the existing reality."

It took me a long time to see that anxiety was affecting me in a major way. Part of the issue was that I was still getting promoted, and I was getting a lot of praise from clients and my managers. But the feedback I was getting would reinforce the unconscious belief that anxiety was the cause of my "success." To maintain that level of anxiety-laden functioning, I had to put in a ton of energy to counteract all that anxiety and stress. I woke up at 6 a.m. to meditate, I had a dedicated prayer practice, I meditated during my lunch break, and meditated in the evenings before bed. In general, I had to spend a lot of time alone to decompress my nervous system. This was sort of sustainable when I was single, more difficult when I got married, and impossible with two kids. But at some point, anxiety-driven functioning catches up to all of us. The cost of is burnout, depression, and a lack of meaningful relationships.

Self-acceptance is always the first step because it gives you space to understand the Anxious Personality. If you're rejecting anxiety, you won't be able to understand it. You won't know why you're anxious, where it came from, or what it's trying to tell you. Anxiety is a signal of something in you that needs attention. Anxiety is the gateway to your healing. It's the gateway to your intrinsic self-confidence. It's the gateway to who you are vs. who you think you should be.

If you're only interested in getting rid of your anxiety, then likely the most effective way of doing that is through medication. There is absolutely no judgment on that, and in many cases I believe that medication is a necessary and welcome support for this kind of work. But if you're reading this book, my guess is that you're interested in learning why you are the way you are. You might question why you struggle so much with anxiety while others don't. And you might question who you really are without anxiety.

I consider myself lucky enough to have discovered the Anxious Personality, and after understanding and dismantling it, know how much more enjoyable, easeful, and carefree life is. This doesn't mean that I don't have challenges or that I don't get anxious from time to time, but anxiety is no longer a constant baseline in my being.

A VISION OF ANXIETY-FREE LIVING

This means that going into client meetings, building relationships, launching a new career all become much, much easier. Without anxiety at the helm, I'm more effective and productive, and it's allowed me to make a few significant changes in my life:

1. Simplicity. When we stop to take stock of what's happening in our inner experience, it's often surprising how much inner chatter there is. Even in the small things like getting chores done, there's all this inner commentary. You can guess that in bigger things like finding a job, switching careers, or getting into a new relationship, anxiety makes it way more complicated than it needs to be. These days, things are much simpler without the system of anxiety to deal with. If I create a course and market it, that's all I'm doing—I'm not worried about how people are going to respond, how they're going to see me, how they might criticize me, whether or not I'm going to survive. All I'm doing is *what* I'm doing.

2. My decisions are no longer based on what other people think. What I decide to do in my life is no

longer dictated by the expectations and pressures of the Anxious Personality's programming, which is incredibly invested in making sure other people aren't upset, critical, or judgmental. (See Chapter 5: The Inner Critic).

3. I've mentioned this already, but disengaging from the Anxious Personality has given me the space to pursue what I love for work. What I do now is so contrary to what the Anxious Personality's programming would have approved of. (Working a corporate job, becoming a doctor, making an inordinate amount of money would have been more aligned with the Anxious Personality's expectations.)

   The work that I do now is satisfying, fulfilling, purpose-driven, service-oriented, and it is a natural expression of my authentic self. If you've thought about a career pivot, you've likely felt a good amount of fear stepping out into such uncertainty because it triggers the Anxious Personality's survival response. It tries to keep you safe, but in doing so, it cripples your passions and joys.

4. I no longer have restless nights because without the Anxious Personality *creating anxiety,* there is a lot more space to simply enjoy life. When the anxiety generator is disabled, it's easier to discern what your priorities are, so you have more time and

clearer boundaries. Because of this work, I've been able to shift from 60+ hour weeks of passionless corporate work to work that I care about. Without all that noise from the Anxious Personality, there's peace, stillness, confidence, and a sense of trust that what is unfolding is going to be good. This is a life-changing orientation.

What I'm really teaching you in these pages is how you can be more of yourself instead of trying so hard to be who you think will get validation or approval from others. This naturally leads to being anxiety-free because when you see through the expectations of the Anxious Personality's programming, you'll find your own definition of what life and success is instead of going along with old expectations that make you miserable.

This isn't just as easy as deciding to be yourself or deciding not to care what other people think about you. There is often healing work that needs to be done, and it is more of a journey than a one-step process. To effectively understand the Anxious Personality, you need to turn your attention inward instead of continually trying to distract yourself with work, social media, or the countless ways we tend to avoid the discomfort of anxiety. All those things are fine, but you won't be able to overcome anxiety without directly looking at it, holding it, and understanding it.

THE MOST POWERFUL THING YOU CAN DO RIGHT NOW

The most powerful thing you can do right now to move toward anxiety-free success is to begin asking why the anxiety you experience is there with curiosity and acceptance. This open-ended curiosity about your anxiety will lead you to healing, understanding, and ultimately freedom. I want to reiterate that there is gold in the anxiety itself! You'll uncover parts of yourself you've lost contact with—your sensitivity, authenticity, your joy, a basic trust in your own value, and a long-forgotten sense of safety that all things are well, including you.

The primary goal I want you to achieve in your life as a result of this book is to have at least one experience of being completely and authentically yourself without being derailed by your anxiety. I want you to see that anxiety is not your natural condition, even though it might have been something that you've lived with for a long time. I want you to know that if you are authentically yourself and free of the Anxious Personality, your long-standing anxiety will no longer affect you in the same way. That not only gives you inner freedom but freedom in your life to pursue the work that you want to pursue, to engage in relationships that you want, and to be intimately in contact with the magic of being alive.

If you intuitively feel in your heart that what I'm saying is true—that anxiety is not *you*—then this book and this work are for you. If you want to know yourself deeply enough that you know to the core of your being that you are valued, safe, and infinitely more than enough, then you'll likely find this framework the right fit. You may have learned how to function with anxiety but know that it isn't optimal, that anxiety is holding you back in a very critical way. You intuitively know the life you are supposed to lead, you intuitively know the work you want to do, and you intuitively know that anxiety-free success is possible. If you're reading this now, you're trusting that intuition, and I hope that as you read, you'll trust yourself even more and discover that being anxiety-free is not only possible but that you can embody a way of being that is most natural to you.

KEY CHAPTER TAKEAWAYS

- The Anxious Personality Framework is most beneficial for people who want to understand the source of their anxiety. This approach isn't a magic pill, but it focuses on dissolving the core causes of anxiety vs. managing its symptoms.

- The first step to addressing any kind of anxiety is reorienting your attitude toward it. Self-acceptance is the key to creating enough inner space to go through the Anxious Personality Framework.

- Life without anxiety is *simple* because there's a lack of inner commentary trying to control how you should be or how others might perceive you. Instead, you just do what you feel guided to do. There's nothing in the way of that, and nothing in the way of you simply showing up as yourself.

CHAPTER 3

THE THREE ANXIETY PATTERNS

A nxiety can be experienced in different ways and in different degrees. Just as being anxiety-free means different things to different people, our experiences of anxiety vary widely, ranging from anxiety applying for a promotion to anxiety about your kid's drop-off at school. But no matter what the situation is, the Anxious Personality generally creates the same recurring **anxiety patterns** for people. These are generally unconscious reactions to the components of the Anxious Personality, and they manifest in certain behaviors that end up defining you and the way you perceive life. You could have adopted one of these patterns or all of these patterns.

There's no judgment about any of these, even though they can end up being problematic. The truth is, they were necessary and brilliant ways that you learned how to cope, survive, and function in your life. But as we've been seeing, there's a cost to having the Anxious Personality run the show. We generally experience anxiety in these patterns, and we're going to explore why in this chapter. My hope is that you'll begin to be curious about these and start to see which ones you tend to favor so you can begin the process of disrupting and loosening their grip on your life. The three main anxiety patterns of the Anxious Personality are:

- Avoidance

- Perfectionism

- People-Pleasing

Each of these anxiety patterns leads to difficulties in our lives. When we avoid taking calls or procrastinating on paying the bills because of underlying anxiety, it keeps us from making progress toward our goals.

When we try to be perfect, attain perfection, or strive for perfection, we often do so at the cost of accepting what about yourself is valuable and worthwhile. With people-pleasing, we sacrifice our own importance and bend over backwards for people, assuming they have more power than we do, making it difficult to set even simple boundaries like how much time you have for a meeting. This doesn't mean you won't have other behavioral patterns where you experience anxiety, so if none of these resonate for you right now, that's okay. It doesn't mean you won't be able to dissolve anxiety. That said, I suggest that you see what does resonate and how it will help you with your own anxiety.

We'll dive into each of these anxiety patterns shortly, but what's more important is seeing how the components of the Anxious Personality work together to cause these behaviors. To refresh your memory, these components are:

- The Inner Critic

- The Sense of Self

- The Core Belief

- The Anxiety Template

It might be helpful to think of the Anxious Personality as a system made up of these different components, and each of these components work together to create a certain output. In the Anxious Personality, the components are put together in a way that outputs anxiety. As we'll see when we cover the Anxiety Template in Chapter 9, there are plenty of different reasons for this, and you likely have already guessed that if the system is creating anxiety, something isn't quite right about how the components are working together.

Each configuration represents a different flavor of how these components come together to form the Anxious Personality and create anxiety. The more invested the Anxious Personality is in trying to protect you, the more rigid these patterns become. This happens because these components form a kind of constellation that gets etched into us, becomes hyper-familiar, and therefore makes it difficult to think that things could be different. I'm sharing these common patterns of the Anxious Personality and their configurations so you can start becoming aware of what configurations resonate with you. But it is also a way to get some understanding about the problems that you might be facing right now.

ANXIETY PATTERN #1: AVOIDANCE

Because anxiety is so uncomfortable, most of us automatically try to get away from it. This has to do with basic pleasure principles that are rooted in our survival instinct, which you'll explore more in Chapter 7. In short, it simply means that our survival is often dependent on going toward what is pleasurable vs. what is not.

There's a big caveat to this, however. **When we avoid uncomfortable or unpleasurable *feelings*, we get into trouble.** These feelings have *everything* to do with long-lasting anxiety. We likely suppressed them because they were too painful at the time, but until we face them again, it's impossible to fully heal from anxiety.

So this configuration of the Anxious Personality has intertwined "avoidance" with "comfort," and it misses the fact that uncomfortable feelings are a part of life and are inevitable. An anxiety-free life doesn't mean that we no longer have uncomfortable feelings. It simply means that the way we relate to discomfort changes dramatically. Anxiety is a symptom of feeling like we are not able or don't want to deal with our challenges. Here are some struggles my clients have come to me with because of this configuration:

- Procrastination

- Binging (watching TV, eating, etc.)

- Withdrawal from social events

- Reluctance to take on projects

What's happening here is that the Anxious Personality is focused on comfort, so it thinks of all these different ways that you could potentially be hurt and tries to avoid them. Instead, it continually opts for comfort. If you can avoid conflict, avoid that presentation, avoid this or that person, avoid that situation, you'll be comfortable...or so the Anxious Personality thinks. It's learned that helping you avoid situations where you might get uncomfortable is the best way to keep you from humiliation, criticism, or whatever flavor of negative feedback you likely received in your early life.

You can see how this can lead to a patterning of trying to be invisible, avoiding the unknown, or limiting your potential. This is why you might be super-competent at work and others see you as skilled and objectively qualified, but you still feel like you have anxiety running through your veins. In the case of avoidance, the Anxious Personality is configured in the following way:

- **Inner Critic Message:** *Don't rock the boat. Don't be noticed.*

- **Sense of Self:** *I am calm and easygoing.*

- **Core Belief:** *I don't matter, I am not important, so I might as well be comfortable.*

- **Anxiety Template:** *What other people want/need is more important than my own wants/needs.*

As you get better at disengaging from the Inner Critic, you'll start to see how often it's telling you to avoid conflict or discomfort. To do its job, the Inner Critic will create and maintain a level of anxiety that causes you to avoid situations where these feelings can come up. The Inner Critic holds the Sense of Self up by telling it, "You're not someone who rocks the boat. You are calm and peaceful, you're someone who goes with the flow." But this Sense of Self has disowned your sense of mattering, making you lose touch with the basic and fundamental right to "take up space." In some cases, this means voicing your opinion or asserting yourself, which is something you likely avoid if you have this type of configuration.

Meanwhile, the Anxiety Template is programmed to follow this groove by automatically assuming that other people are more important than yourself—other people have more say, their opinions matter more, you just have to go along with what everyone else decides. The tension between the Sense of Self and your Core Belief creates an underlying feeling of constant anxiety. Before dismantling the Anxious Personality, you'll unconsciously experience the pressure this dynamic creates—you unconsciously have feelings about disowning your sense of mattering but are constricted to the Inner Critic's main message of avoiding discomfort.

For those of you who have this configuration of avoidance, dismantling the Anxious Personality will mean creating enough inner space for you to reconnect with a sense of basic trust and the direct experience that you do matter, that it's okay to take up space and assert yourself, and that discomfort is not the end of the world. You may rationally understand that, but experientially, the rest of "you" thinks all will be lost if life gets too rocky.

But with enough understanding and self-awareness, the Anxious Personality will "loosen," and the real you, having access to your own sense of mattering, can emerge. You might be able to see how an anxiety-free life can also emerge naturally when you no longer have the Anxious Personality convincing you that you don't matter. When you're able to take up space and comfortably assert yourself, you no longer avoid situations that might have debilitated you before.

ANXIETY PATTERN #2: PERFECTIONISM

Another core pattern for the Anxious Personality is perfectionism. When anxiety makes us feel insecure, it's natural for us to try and find security and reassurance. With perfectionism, the Anxious Personality believes that if things are perfect, we will be valued and all things will be well. So the Anxious Personality drives us to be perfect in everything we do, whether that's making sure every detail in a presentation is just right or that you pack the kids' lunches in exactly the right way. In other words, it's *not* okay to make any mistakes.

There's obviously a cost to this. Here are some common scenarios where my clients struggle with perfectionism:

- Inability to make progress on projects or hit deadlines.

- Burnout due to overwork.

- Difficulty delegating responsibilities at work (impacting leaders or managers).

- Extreme self-criticism after calls, interviews, meetings, or conversations.

The unconscious thinking behind this pattern often goes something like this: "If I work hard enough, I won't be criticized, shamed, or experience unwanted or painful feedback." Anxiety is built right into that driving and striving for perfection. This isn't to say that we shouldn't work on improving or perfecting a vocation or skill—it's just a different thing when the motivation for perfection comes from the Anxious Personality. But it's not enough to simply change your thinking and say, "Okay, I'm probably spending too much time trying to make things perfect. I'll stop now." As we've said in the Introduction, anxiety is embedded into the entire personality structure, and it's by understanding the different components of the Anxious Personality that you'll be able to dismantle it.

The configuration of the Anxious Personality in the case of perfectionism looks like this:

- **Inner Critic Message:** *You need to do things perfectly, better, and without mistakes.*

- **Sense of Self:** *I am an achiever.*

- **Core Belief:** *I am not intrinsically valuable and worthy.*

- **Anxiety Template:** *Other people are the ones who judge whether or not I am valuable.*

Why did the Anxious Personality get configured in this particular way? You'll get a chance to dig into that in Chapter 7 as we trace the Anxious Personality's origin story back to your own history. Generally though, whether you are aware of it or not, perfectionism forms because something was missing in your early environment—in this case, you likely experienced some lack of support for your true and authentic nature. Because this intrinsic value was missed and not mirrored to some degree, you naturally felt a sense that something wasn't right or harmonious in the environment. There's a distinct sense of helplessness that you feel in that experience, and instead of feeling helpless, The Anxious Personality's response to such an experience is to believe that have to "do something" and do it well instead of relaxing and trusting that the environment will come to meet you with warmth, support, love and nurturance.

This is the first sign of perfectionism and where the Inner Critic can get extremely harsh. It will constantly push you to do things better, more correctly, with more efficiency, etc. But it will never be good enough for the Inner Critic. I'm always amazed when my clients are so surprised after completing the Inner Critic Inventory (Chapter 11) and getting in touch with this particular flavor of the Inner Critic. They say, "Oh, no wonder I'm feeling anxious all the time!" I always affirm that with a big, YES! Anyone would feel anxious if they had someone constantly telling them that what they are doing isn't good enough.

But that is actually what is happening. The tricky thing about this configuration of the Anxious Personality is that the Inner Critic also acts like a coach. It will approve of you when you "do things right" or "do things well." But it will also hammer you with criticism as a way to motivate you. Really, it's trying to keep you safe, but as we've discussed, the cost is a constant, underlying feeling of anxiety that never turns off.

So the Sense of Self becomes about being good at things, being able to accomplish a lot, being able to be better than others, having a coveted kind of skillset, etc. But what is hiding underneath that Sense of Self is the belief that you actually aren't valuable at all. It's only through doing things perfectly or "being" perfect that you have value. In fact, for many of my clients who have this configuration, they don't feel like they are worth anything if they haven't achieved perfection.

The main problem with the pattern of perfectionism is that it puts your sense of value outside of yourself. If you have no sense of the value of *you* simply being *you*, then you'll look for others to validate your worthiness, which is exactly what the Anxiety Template is set up to do in this configuration. When you give others the power to judge whether or not you are worthy or valuable, of course you would feel anxiety. What if someone doesn't approve of you? What if someone really doesn't like you? What if you say something that unintentionally hurts someone?

I hope you are starting to see how the different components of the Anxious Personality create an internal tension that we experience as anxiety. By using the Direct Inquiry Method, you systematically identify the various aspects of the Inner Critic, the Sense of Self, the Core Belief, and the Anxiety Template of a particular configuration. In the case of perfectionism, Inner Critic work (Chapter 7) is really, really important and takes quite a bit of time to master because its messages can be so harsh.

But when you effectively distance yourself from the Anxious Personality's perfectionistic messages, you'll experience a new inner freedom and actually come to know that you are in fact a wonderful, worthy, and priceless individual.

ANXIETY PATTERN #3: PEOPLE-PLEASING

Another configuration of the Anxious Personality results in people-pleasing. A certain amount of give and take is necessary to be in a relationship, but people-pleasing is about adjusting and changing ourselves to make sure other people approve of us. One way of thinking about people-pleasing is to notice how uncomfortable you are with the possibility that somebody else might be upset with you, criticize you, or be angry with you based on what you say or do. So people-pleasers tend to either morph or change who they are according to who they think others want them to be.

This becomes a problematic pattern for people with this particular configuration because you end up spending a lot of time thinking about how you should be instead of simply being how you are. If you're constantly worrying about how others might react, then the only thing you can really do is to freeze, which is exactly what happens when we over-analyze and over-anticipate how other people will respond to us. My clients who have come to me with this people-pleasing characteristic find themselves struggling the most in the following situations:

- When they are making transitions (career pivots, relationship changes, etc.)

- When they have to set strong boundaries.

- When they have to make a decision (especially as an authority figure).

- When they want to share their opinion or post on social media.

- When they need to communicate what they want or what they need.

- When they need to give a public presentation (it's impossible to make *everyone* happy, so the Anxious Personality freaks out!)

As a result, people-pleasers find themselves far from anxiety-free functioning because they have lost contact with their own strength and power. This is closely related to a sense of autonomy—that you are okay on your own, that others don't need to like you, and that you are strong enough to handle whatever situation comes your way. This people-pleasing configuration is set up in this way:

- **Inner Critic Message:** *Know what's expected of you and do it without fail.*

- **Sense of Self:** *I am dependable and loyal.*

- **Core Belief:** *I cannot trust others to be safe.*

- **Anxiety Template:** *Other people (or the world itself) will hurt me, so I need to protect myself.*

The key to understanding this configuration is that it's all about security. This type of Anxious Personality continually seeks security and looks for it by knowing what's expected and covering all the bases. This leads to a lot of energy going toward anticipating all the things that can go wrong. This configuration creates doubt and a constant questioning of "what if?" *What if the project doesn't go well? What if my partner doesn't like the present I got? What if my date doesn't like what I'm wearing?* This kind of catastrophic thinking is common for this anxiety pattern, and it's easy to see how it prevents you from stepping out and doing not just new endeavors, but daily tasks also. To the anxious mind, there is always something to worry about!

The Inner Critic message in this configuration does everything it can to figure out how to keep you secure and safe, and it does this by proactively finding out what's expected from the people around you. The rationale is, "If I'm doing what's expected of me, others will be happy and I will be safe." So the Anxious Personality here develops a Sense of Self that is dependable, loyal, and steadfast. These are great qualities, but before you go through the process of understanding the Anxious Personality, they are underpinned by a Core Belief that others will hurt you in some way.

This gets transferred onto the world, so the programming of the Anxiety Template is geared toward thinking the world itself is unsafe and that the best way to stay safe is to make sure people around you are "pleased" with you. It's a brilliant survival mechanism, but like all the configurations of the Anxious Personality we've talked about so far, it comes at a cost. Eventually, you begin to feel that all the life is sucked out of you because life itself is dynamic, so there's always a degree of uncertainty about it. When we focus on what can or will go wrong with life as a way to find safety, we limit how much of life we are able to take.

As you begin to understand and dismantle the components of this particular configuration, you'll begin to experience a kind of inner security that has nothing to do with others. When you disengage from the Inner Critic, you'll question why you've automatically tended to put others first or prioritize their needs over yours. As you get in touch with inner security, you find less and less pull to be "dependable" or "always there." You'll see that things won't fall apart if you let go of people-pleasing. As this sense of inner security grows, even your Core Belief will begin to shift. You'll no longer be so convinced that the world is full of threats. Instead, you'll be able to see that the world is full of opportunity, and that these opportunities are exciting and expansive.

DISSOLVING THE ANXIETY PATTERNS

This might be a truth that's hard for you buy into right now, but it's absolutely possible to dissolve these patterns, even if they've been with you for a lifetime. When we bring enough awareness and understanding of what causes these patterns, we also start to see where the original disconnection to the essential qualities of power, confidence, value, self-worth, love, and acceptance occurred.

Noticing these anxiety patterns becomes a gateway to a kind of natural gift or superpower. It's as if losing connection to these essential qualities and *reconnecting* with them makes us more *attuned* to them. They become like "anxiety superpowers" that we know more intimately because we've gone through the process of understanding them. You'll see in the next chapter that the Anxious Personality Framework isn't about willfully changing any of these patterns. They dissolve because when we reconnect with our authentic nature, we don't need to rely on these patterns anymore. In Part 2, you'll learn about the inner workings of each component and how they work together to create an anxiety-driven worldview that actually isn't true.

SELF-ASSESSMENT

Which anxiety pattern do you tend toward the most? Read each statement and rate yourself on a scale of 1 - 10, 1 being "Completely Disagree" and 10 being "Completely Agree."

	STATEMENT	RATING
1	I make a concerted effort not to draw attention to myself.	
2	I tend to have trouble getting things started.	
3	I actively look for things that will provide me comfort.	
4	I often think it isn't worth the effort to express my own views or needs in a group.	
5	If I'm not contributing in some way, I feel out of sorts.	
6	Although other people see me as competent, I don't really feel that I am.	
7	I tend to spend a lot of time getting the details right so others won't criticize me.	
8	I tend not to ask people for help, even though I can really use it.	
9	I'm not really comfortable being the leader or holding power.	

10	I tend to look for potential dangers and try my best to avoid them.
11	When I'm doing something new, I prefer to have someone doing it with me, especially if they have some expertise.
12	I prefer having stable, secure relationships over meeting new people.

Results:

The Avoidance Pattern: Score for #1-4 _____

The Perfectionism Pattern: Score for #5-8 _____

The People-Pleasing Pattern: Score for #9-12_____

How to interpret your scores:

Whatever category you scored the highest is the anxiety pattern that you likely rely on more. Note: any of these patterns can show up as they are all outputs of the Anxious Personality, so you could score high in any one of these patterns or all three of them. Once you have your score, see if you can notice when these patterns show up in your day-to-day life. As you become aware of them and learn about the components of the Anxious Personality in Part 2, you'll be able to disrupt or disengage from these patterns more easily.

KEY CHAPTER TAKEAWAYS

- There are three primary anxiety patterns that the Anxious Personality exhibits.

- The components of the Anxious Personality have a slightly different "flavor" for each anxiety pattern. Understanding these components will help disrupt these patterns and bring you closer to reconnecting to different essential qualities i.e. a sense of mattering, value, power, and confidence.

- The Avoidance Pattern shows up when we avoid feeling our anxiety and don't feel like we have the capacity to fully engage with the things we need to do in our lives. The primary disconnection of the Avoidance Pattern is an inner sense of mattering and support.

- The Perfection Pattern shows up when we believe that our value is dependent on how others perceive us. It's exhibited in behaviors like overwork and self-criticism. The primary disconnection of the Perfection Pattern is an intrinsic sense of value and self-worth.

- The People-Pleasing Pattern shows up when we believe that the world is threatening in some way and it's imperative to find security and safety. As a result, we try to accommodate and please others to create a false sense of security. The primary disconnection of the People-Pleasing Pattern is a sense of inner security.

CHAPTER 4

COMMON APPROACHES TO ANXIETY AND THEIR LIMITATIONS

I hope it's starting to become clear that there's a difference between "personality" and who you really are. This isn't a new concept. Thousands of years of ancient wisdom teachings have pointed to a "false personality" and that the path of enlightenment is to realize your true nature. In other words, if we can let go of who we think we are, then we can simply "be." In modern times, these teachings have formed the basis for the popularity of the Enneagram, which categorizes nine personality types and their patterns. In addition to that, modern psychologists have built on Sigmund Freud's work and advanced his theories on the personality with ego psychology and depth psychology.

As I mentioned in the introduction, the Anxious Personality Framework uses these principles and focuses particularly on personality types that experience anxiety as a core part of their identity. I think it's worth elaborating on the difference between the false personality and the true self because it is so important to the way the Anxious Personality Framework helps free us from anxiety.

Anxiety is not a new issue, but I believe that approaches that do not have a full understanding of the components that create anxiety miss out on the deeper and more comprehensive layers of transformation. In this chapter, I want to lay out common approaches or philosophies to anxiety and provide an explanation on why they work but also why they are limited. I hope this will help clarify my framework and why I think it's so important to go through and understand each component of the Anxious Personality and how they are configured.

COMMON APPROACH #1: "Shift Your Mindset"

"Shifting your mindset" has become part of the mainstream culture of self-care and positive mental health. It works, but in my experience, it's a band-aid kind of solution. It's true that deliberately changing your thoughts, especially if you are prone to negative or catastrophizing thoughts, will help reduce the level of anxiety you might be experiencing. After all, the mind is a powerful thing. In many cases, practicing positive self-talk counteracts the personality's tendency toward negativity bias, which is our brain's wiring to put more emphasis on negative events or thoughts.

The problem is that changing your thoughts alone without understanding where the negative thoughts originate from doesn't ever address the root of "trait anxiety" or the kind of anxiety that's embedded in the personality. I personally and systematically went through a number of positive mindset shifts in my early attempts to get rid of anxiety and depression. It was great. I had a ritual of going through the Power Cards of Louise Hay, one of the pioneers who made the "new thought" movement more mainstream. I didn't know it at the time, but I completely suppressed and compartmentalized any thoughts I deemed "negative." It was helpful at the time, but later I couldn't help but intuitively sense that I was ignoring a very large part of myself.

It turns out I was right. The old programming of the Anxious Personality was still running and creating anxiety—only I was ignoring it by constantly putting a positive spin on things. What I actually ended up doing—and I witness this with many people who have tried **approaches that prioritize change over understanding**—is a kind of bypassing of my full self. Another way to say this is I became one-dimensional. I only allowed "positive" things, and I relegated feelings like anxiety, depression, sadness, and anger to the unconscious, or as Jungian therapists like to call it, the "shadow" side.

You might guess that anything we repress for that long will always resurface (and generally with more intensity). In other words, out of sight doesn't necessarily mean that it doesn't exist. What lives in our shadow will tend to push up toward the surface until we deal with them. So, while this mindset shift approach worked for a number of years, all it did was create a polished "persona" on top of the Anxious Personality that was already there. I came across as happy, relaxed, confident, and carefree—but it never felt authentic because underneath was a ton of anxiety of being "found out." Those of you whose anxiety is intertwined with imposter syndrome will know this experience well.

Because I hadn't learned about the components of the Anxious Personality, all the transformation I experienced was primarily in the realm of "magical thinking" or prayer. When I felt happier, I had no idea why, and I certainly couldn't reproduce this feeling. I didn't know then that prayer and mindset shifts were ways to temporarily pause the Anxious Personality. The problem was that I was still identified with the Anxious Personality. **I still thought of myself as an anxious person and was trying to get rid of anxiety through mindset shifts.**

To understand the Anxious Personality is to understand that your operating system is programmed to create anxiety. Trying to reprogram it with new mindsets is like trying to write new code without erasing the old code. It can be done, but it's not complete. Why? Because the dissolution of the Anxious Personality comes when your conscious mind understands the subconscious mind. Another way to say this is that healing only comes when we know what specifically needs to be healed, and although anxiety may seem vague and mysterious, it's actually very specific.

COMMON APPROACH #2: "Fake It 'Till You Make It"

I see this kind of conventional wisdom in the professional realm, where people will suggest a "fake it 'till you make it" or "step out of your comfort zone" approach. The rationale behind this is that once you get enough practice at something, your anxiety will fade as you build skill. The main misunderstanding here is that it misses the difference between *"state anxiety"* and *"trait anxiety,"* which I talked about in Chapter 1. State anxiety is anxiety that can occur when you're learning something new, or you've started a new job. Yes, there's a degree of discomfort at doing something new and as it becomes more familiar, the anxiety fades.

But for people who have an Anxious Personality, it doesn't matter as much how "good" they are at something because the anxiety is a byproduct of the personality system. In fact, that is where the phenomenon of imposter syndrome gets so challenging. Someone who is objectively well-qualified, high achieving, and competent can still internally experience an unhealthy level of anxiety. Furthermore, if you have an Anxious Personality, stepping out of your comfort zone often triggers more constriction and stress. Healing for people with an Anxious Personality is not about stepping out of your comfort zone, it's about dissolving the boundaries of your comfort zone so continual growth isn't stressful.

I used to believe in the conventional wisdom of getting uncomfortable in order to grow i.e. "comfort is the enemy of growth" and it was initially how I was first introduced to coaching. But I've come to see that this perspective stems from our hyper-capitalistic worldview, where we have confused being free from anxiety with laziness and familiarity. **Growth can, in fact, be effortless, smooth, AND comfortable**—even in circumstances that are unfamiliar or challenging. You only have to understand the artificial boundaries of what we've historically called our "comfort zone." These are all the unsaid, unconscious rules that bind us to the Anxious Personality.

When I quit my job of 10+ years and embarked on a new journey to build a service to support people in their journey to overcome anxiety, stress, and imposter syndrome, you might think that this would have been anxiety-provoking. I have two kids under six. Our stockpiled savings ran out after 9 months because we live in one of the most expensive places in California. I'd gotten ghosted more times in the first year than I had in the last ten. I wouldn't say it was easy, but after having worked through the different components of the Anxious Personality, I've become more skilled at recognizing arbitrary beliefs, understanding them, and removing them so in each situation I encounter, I feel clear, spacious and in contact with myself. So what I have learned is that comfort isn't the enemy of growth. Our unawareness of what is keeping us tied to what is familiar is. You can still grow without becoming aware of these inner boundaries, but that is unnecessarily uncomfortable and ultimately not as effective.

COMMON APPROACH #3: "More Mindfulness"

I will never undervalue the practice of mindfulness. I am, after all, a certified mindfulness trainer! But in my experience, it isn't enough to overcome anxiety. Rather, mindfulness is a starting point to being able to understand the Anxious Personality. Much of the mainstream mindfulness approach is based on the concept of neuroplasticity and the idea that you can change the physiology of the brain with enough practice. But research is now coming out that debunks the initial claims of how much practice is needed to change the brain. In short: it's a lot!

The widely accepted definition of mindfulness is "paying attention to the present moment without judgment." The problem is that when the Anxious Personality is present, it's impossible to do this. The Anxious Personality judges each moment *constantly*, perceiving reality in a fearful way, trying to control the present moment, or being scared of the many moments to come. Without understanding or even being aware of the Anxious Personality and its components, practicing mindfulness isn't enough. You can spend 1,000 hours meditating and feel anxiety-free during those hours. The problem is that once you are back in your life, all the things that trigger the Anxious Personality go into full effect. I can't tell you how many times I opened my eyes from a blissful, transcendent meditation where I felt completely ecstatic, free, deeply still and peaceful – only to open one email to have all of it completely vanish.

But the missing ingredient that we often forget is understanding. And this is where the Western approach of psychology and the focus on individual experience and functioning is so useful. Without understanding, the components of the Anxious Personality—our self-criticism, our expectations, our fears, our defenses, our self-sabotage—never really dissolve. Here's what I mean:

- Let's say I notice that I am all of a sudden tense in my shoulders.

- I stay with the tension and notice that it's not just my shoulders that are tense. It's my jaw, and there's some constriction in my throat and belly.

- I can sense some sadness in my throat, and there's some sense of emotional pain in my jaw.

- I sense in my belly there's a feeling of deficiency, like the bottom is going to fall out, and I notice there's a feeling of desperation and helplessness.

All of this is possible through mindfulness—the non-judgmental awareness of the present moment. If you look at our tendency to run from any kind of discomfort, you can see why mindfulness is so important. But let's add the element of understanding and see what happens:

- Tension in my shoulders, jaw, and throat. I can see that there's some constriction that is happening in my being, and I know from the Anxious Personality's Anxiety Template that I tend to think that I need to protect myself from others. What or whom am I protecting myself from?

- Sadness in my throat, emotional pain in my jaw. Why is there sadness there? What is the pain about? Oh, I can sense that I feel as if I'm alone, that I have to do things on my own.

- Belly feeling of desperation and helplessness. What is the helplessness about? Why is it there? Oh...I feel like I'm 13 again and my dad just criticized me for not being capable or having any common sense, and this desperation in my belly has this scary message in it about not having what it takes.

- When I allow this feeling, I also start to feel compassion for my 13-year-old self. Tears come and this tension I originally felt releases in waves of pain that had been frozen in my shoulders.

- After the crying ends, what I feel in the space is a natural kind of support and holding, as well as a sense of inner security. I feel as if something that had been there for a long time was lifted.

I hope this gives you a sense of how the experience is different with the added ingredient of understanding. You might also ask, what's the point of understanding all of this? It's because the understanding gets us closer to healing, it's what supports you to finally be able to let go and surrender—not just temporarily, but forever. That particular piece of code simply disappears, and what is left is space to simply be yourself and in contact with your inherent nature.

In the case above, if I am able to be mindful of the feeling of desperation and helplessness and understand that this is from unresolved trauma from my history, I may be able to sense what is also present—which may be essential support, compassion, love, worthiness, etc. This is the power of The Anxious Personality Framework. It doesn't provide techniques to help you cope with anxiety. Understanding and dismantling the Anxious Personality frees you from its programming altogether. It's the difference between "managing symptoms" and "healing the root cause."

COMMON APPROACH #4:
"Improve Yourself"

This might seem like an odd inclusion, given that this book by nature is a self-help book. But it's related to not having a thorough understanding of how personal transformation actually works. Self-improvement is great, but do you actually know what the "self" is? What most people believe is the "self" is actually the Anxious Personality. Why is this important? Because without knowing how the components of the Anxious Personality work, it's really easy to have the Anxious Personality co-op your self-improvement progress.

Here's an example: Let's say you've found that meditation is a good way to manage your anxiety and you've committed to do it every day. For a while, this is really good and you feel the positive effects of daily meditation. But you're not yet aware of the Inner Critic and its role in the Anxious Personality, and naturally after a few weeks of meditating you start to feel tired of it. So what happens? The Anxious Personality takes your experience of meditation and runs it through the old components:

- The Inner Critic comes in and starts to say, "You should be meditating more. Why aren't you? How come you can't be more disciplined? This is good for you, but you can't seem to keep it up."

- This triggers the Sense of Self. "I need to do this perfectly. After all, I'm working on myself and this is what's going to get me free of anxiety once and for all!"

- This in turn triggers the Core Belief of "I need to be perfect to have value." You start to think that you're not doing it perfectly or enough, and that you'll never actually be free of anxiety.

- When you then talk to your coach, mentor, or teacher, you feel bad about yourself because there's so much pressure to "keep it up." Even if your coach is kind and supportive, the anxiety is already there, and the Anxious Personality thinks that your coach knows how bad you are!

By its very nature, the Anxious Personality will take any experience and turn it into anxiety, even meditation! But when you are aware of the components of the Anxious Personality, you start to see how the system works. The more aware of it you are, the more you can dismantle it. Make no mistake: the Anxious Personality is sneaky. Inherently, it lives in the unconscious and under the radar. It's only by learning how to recognize it that we can truly do anything about it.

COMMON APPROACH #5:
"Just Deal with It" or "Make an Action Plan"

I wish I didn't have to address this, but I've found that in many of my discovery calls with potential clients that many of them have been told that anxiety is just something they have to "deal with." Or they give them an action plan to change anxious behaviors and expect that to solve a lifetime of anxiety. This kind of advice is usually given by people who don't have the same personality structure and don't have the same experience with anxiety as someone with an Anxious Personality. To them, "just dealing with it" is generally possible because the components of their personality structure are configured really differently. For them, their Inner Critic might be protecting them by shutting down or numbing their anxiety, so the Sense of Self becomes pseudo-confident or pseudo-strong.

In actuality, everyone with a personality structure will experience anxiety, but for the Anxious Personality structure, the components orbit around anxiety, whereas other personalities might orbit around issues of mistrust or not belonging. So yes, just "dealing with it" is possible for a while, but eventually it will lead to burnout because living with chronic anxiety is not a pleasant experience—and it's not natural to our authentic being.

Like I've mentioned before, "dealing with it" is like dragging an anchor continually holding your boat back and not doing anything about it. Yes, you can move if you run the motor harder, but eventually the engine will burn out. To me, it's much easier to figure out why the anchor is there and remove it. Efforting, striving, and pushing only makes anxiety worse for the Anxious Personality. Another analogy I like to use is that dealing with anxiety is like having a pair of Chinese finger cuffs. The more you try to get out of it, the more it tightens its hold.

THE MISSING KEY: DISSOLVING ALL FOUR COMPONENTS

Many approaches to self-improvement or personal development cover one or two of the components of the Anxious Personality, but without a more thorough understanding of all four components and how they work together, the Anxious Personality will stick around. If you only focus on the initial layers of the Inner Critic, you'll think that you've conquered the obvious self-criticisms but not realize how the Inner Critic "holds up" a Sense of Self that is overwhelmed and fearful all the time. I'll add that a lot of mainstream coaching around the Inner Critic mostly focuses on mindset changes, which in my experience doesn't effectively help someone understand the Inner Critic enough to dissolve it.

Similarly, if you try to will yourself to improve your Sense of Self, you won't experience the real healing that happens when you see through the Core Belief you've been carrying around. If you don't experience how your Core Belief is false, then you won't be able to contact or realize true inner security and safety. And if you don't adequately become aware of your Anxiety Template, the Anxious

Personality will automatically show up whenever you interact with someone that triggers that template. But if you have a strong understanding of all four components of the Anxious Personality, the system begins to dissolve and stops running, which means it stops creating anxiety by default. You don't need to "effort" at all—the system simply stops because it's no longer needed.

KEY CHAPTER TAKEAWAYS

- Many common approaches that try to change or shift the subconscious never get to the root of anxiety because anxiety is deeply ingrained in the personality.

- Focusing on behavior change helps to manage symptoms of anxiety by trying to implement healthier coping strategies, but behavior change won't heal anxiety. This is because anxiety doesn't come from behavior, it comes from the components of the personality.

- Trying to create a "new and improved" version of yourself takes you further away from the root cause of anxiety. It also takes you further from authentic self-confidence, self-worth, intrinsic value, and inner power, which are the qualities of presence that dissolve anxiety and its components.

- Focusing on working through just one of the components of the Anxious Personality won't dissolve anxiety completely because all four components work together to create and maintain anxiety in your system.

- The key to dissolving anxiety is to understand how it shows up in the underlying components of the personality. When we have enough understanding, we lose our identification with being an "anxious person" and are able to embody inner qualities of value, worth, confidence, power, security, and support.

PART TWO

UNDERSTANDING THE ANXIOUS PERSONALITY

CHAPTER 5

THE DIRECT INQUIRY METHOD

U nderstanding the Anxious Personality sounds like a nice idea, but at this point, you're probably eager to get to the "how." If the Anxious Personality is a prison that keeps you locked up with your anxiety, how do you get out of it? I often asked myself this question as I read books about personal development, enlightenment, or spiritual practices. I experienced the teachers, gurus, and prominent coaches of the world saying, "Think this way" or "This is how it is."

But even as I attempted to change my thinking and even as I got validation of my own transformation from these same teachers, I always felt that there was much more underneath the surface that I wasn't seeing. And certainly I always felt that subtle (and sometimes not so subtle) layer of anxiety. If the majority of the Anxious Personality's components are often underneath the surface of our awareness, how do you see what's there? We can't simply just decide to identify these different components and say, "Okay, I'm done with all that now."

If our goal is to try to understand the Inner Critic, the Sense of Self, the Core Belief, and the Anxiety Template as best we can, but all they are buried in our unconscious, then we need a tool to be able to easily and more quickly excavate these unconscious messages and beliefs. **The Direct Inquiry Method is that tool.**

Inquiry in general is the process of exploring the various threads of what is true about any given topic (like anxiety). In the realm of personal development, inquiry helps us unravel our relationship with our issues and roadblocks so we can see them more clearly. Dr. Gabor Mate, renowned author and psychologist, created the term, "compassionate inquiry," which is a psychotherapeutic method that "unveils the level of consciousness, mental climate, hidden assumptions, implicit memories and body states that form the real message that words both express and conceal." While this is a great approach, general inquiry can be meandering and take a lot of time, especially if you're not practiced at following the thread of truth. You may not be used to navigating the "hidden assumptions" that lie beneath our awareness. It's particularly difficult if you haven't done much mindfulness or meditation training because you can endlessly jump from one thought to another and not get anywhere.

That's why I created the Direct Inquiry Method, which is a systematic way of inquiring into the specific components of the Anxious Personality we've been talking about. The Direct

Inquiry Method consists of two primary techniques, repeating questions and inventories.

REPEATING QUESTIONS

This is where a question is asked and answered repeatedly, usually for a given amount of time. The questions can be answered in one of two possible ways:

1. Right off the top of your head.

2. Using the previous answer as a springboard to take the next answer deeper.

To illustrate how this works, I'll use a specific example of a repeating question inquiry I use with my clients to help identify hidden Inner Critic messages.

- I ask the client, "How does the Inner Critic judge your anger?"

- The client responds with whatever comes up for them, "It says anger isn't safe."

- I then say, "Thank you," and ask again, "How does the Inner Critic judge your anger?"

- The client again responds with whatever comes up in the moment, "It says that if I get angry, bad things will happen."

- I say thank you again and repeat the question.

The process is repeated until time expires, usually ten or fifteen minutes.

I want to point out a few things about this example. The first is that the way the question is formed is extremely important. We are directly inquiring about a specific dimension of the Inner Critic, which in this case is how the Inner Critic judges our anger. It is not an open-ended inquiry about self-criticism. Instead, we are being very targeted about excavating the hidden rules the Inner Critic has for you. In my framework, we use the Direct Inquiry Method to explore different dimensions of messages from the Inner Critic, which you'll have a chance to do in the self-assessments that are in Part 3. These dimensions are places in us that the Inner Critic tends to have the strongest messages about, and when it does, creates the anxiety that impacts our behavior and shapes the Sense of Self.

When you first begin to respond to these repeating questions, you'll likely respond with the most obvious answers that come up in your head. But the power of repeating questions is that by the 10th time you're asked the question, you may have run out of easy answers and you'll have to let the answers begin to come from your unconscious. Like a very good drill, each turn gets you deeper and deeper toward the truth.

Generally, repeating questions are done in a 1:1 private session, but the exercise is also quite powerful through journaling. In the journaling format, you simply ask yourself the question and write down your response, starting a new line for each time you ask yourself the question. I've included this format in Part 3 of the book.

INVENTORIES

The second technique to the Direct Inquiry Method uses inventories, which is a way to organize the insights we gain from the repeating question exercises. Organizing your insights gives you the opportunity to easily identify patterns of the Anxious Personality and how its components work together to create and sustain anxiety. In our system, we take an inventory for each of the components of the Anxious Personality:

- The Inner Critic Inventory
- Sense of Self Inventory
- Core Beliefs Inventory
- Anxiety Template Inventory

After you complete these inventories, we'll be able to identify the most prominent patterns and create a map of the Anxious Personality to help you begin to understand these components. The more we become conscious and self-aware of these patterns, the less of a hold they'll have on us.

The purpose of the Direct Inquiry Method is to systemize the process of identifying the different components of the Anxious Personality, which is usually hidden in the unconscious. I often describe the Direct Inquiry Method as a specialized tool. It's the difference between going to see your primary care doctor versus going to see a specialist. A general practitioner can help you diagnose issues, but sometimes you need to go to a specialist for certain things.

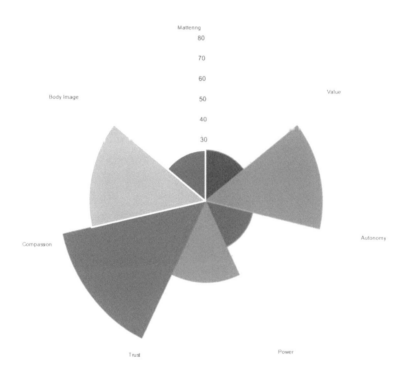

Example of an Anxious Personality "Map." Each category score is determined by a self-rating based on repeating question responses.

This Direct Inquiry Method specializes in getting to the root of anxiety, so it's a more surgical approach. It's designed to ask specific questions in our inquiry sessions that elicit understanding of a particular component or insight, and these insights build on each other in a way where you can understand and let go of the Anxious Personality. Because the Direct Inquiry Method is systemized, you know exactly where you are in the process, which supports a kind of empowerment. *You* are the one that is getting the insights. *You* are the one reconnecting with what is inside. *You* are the one that is discovering the gold. In Part 3, you'll have an opportunity to use the Direct Inquiry Method and experience what it's like to build insight in this way.

IDEAL CONDITIONS FOR EFFECTIVE DIRECT INQUIRY

For the Direct Inquiry Method to work effectively, you'll need to approach it with a willingness to be present. This requires a combination of attitudes toward finding out what is true for you and what makes up the Anxious Personality.

Acceptance

Discovering what is in the Anxious Personality can be like opening up a closet that you haven't looked into for a long time. The Direct Inquiry Method is like taking each object out of the closet and seeing what it is, and usually it'll seem like things get a lot messier before they get cleaner. This takes a certain level of acceptance, even if you don't necessarily like what you see. You might see that there's a certain level of masquerading you've been doing. You might see painful memories or come into contact with old hurts.

All of this is important in understanding the Anxious Personality and eventually dismantling it. But without acceptance, you end up putting these things back in the closet again. **A word of advice: You can't selectively choose your insights.** What Direct Inquiry reveals is what you get, so it's helpful to trust that whatever you discover will support your growth and transformation.

Open-Ended Curiosity

It's one thing to take an object out of the closet and it's another thing to be curious about it. Where did this thing come from? How old is it? What actually is it? What does it do? Open-ended curiosity spurs deeper questions about what you discover about the Anxious Personality. This kind of curiosity often asks why things are the way they are and wants to deepen your understanding about an insight. For example, if you discover that your Inner Critic is often telling you that you're not good enough, open-ended curiosity might ask, *Where did that message come from? Why is it saying that? When did that voice start?*

Steadfastness

The process of Direct Inquiry might seem daunting at first, and going through repeating question exercises might also seem laborious. Steadfastness doesn't mean pushing yourself through any of this, but it does mean staying with whatever comes up. You might come up against boredom, but instead of pushing through it, you can be steadfast in staying with the experience of boredom. You might come up against fear, but instead of avoiding it, you can be steadfast in being with the fear. This not only builds a muscle of being present, which in itself will help with your anxiety, it will allow you to have deeper and richer insights with Direct Inquiry.

Staying Present

If at this point, you're telling yourself, "Oh, I don't have those things so I can't do this," don't worry. All of this comes down to being with yourself and asking what is here. This sounds simple but is actually pretty hard to pull off if you're not used to it. Most people aren't actually "here" and fully paying attention to their experience. Most are thinking about the future, thinking about the past, worrying about this or that thing, focused on their to-do list, etc. But even if you are "not here," it's a quick pivot to noticing where you are now. As long as you're moving in the direction of being present, you'll eventually cultivate these attitudes of acceptance, curiosity, and steadfastness. In Part 3, you'll learn about specific practices to help cultivate these attitudes so you can more easily understand and dissolve the Anxious Personality.

NEXT STEPS

Obviously, the Direct Inquiry Method is easier said than done. In a lot of ways, this kind of work requires guidance from somebody who has been through this experience and is able to help you navigate the terrain. When we start, our unconscious tendencies to avoid, hide, or ignore things about the Anxious Personality are pretty strong. That's where a guide can help. In my one-on-one sessions, I'm not just asking a client the question, I'm helping them see where they are shut down to curiosity, or where they are having trouble accepting something, or how the Inner Critic has just judged them. It might also be difficult to tell whether or not you're in the right place to use Direct Inquiry, since the starting point for Direct Inquiry to be effective really is a baseline capacity to be present, so it's helpful when you've already established a degree of mental focus and ability to be aware of your thoughts and emotions.

If you feel like you are ready and want to dive into the framework, feel free to jump into the next four chapters, which explain each component of the Anxious Personality and how to dissolve it using Direct Inquiry. There's a lot to unpack, so take a deep breath and take a moment to be where you are. When you're ready, onward!

KEY CHAPTER TAKEAWAYS

- The Direct Inquiry Method is the primary tool to gain the insights needed to understand the different components of the Anxious Personality.

- Different uses of Direct Inquiry are repeating questions, which are designed to steadily deepen inquiry beyond the conscious mind. Another method is reflective journaling to specific prompts about various aspects of anxiety.

- In order for Direct Inquiry to be effective, a foundation of presence and support needs to be established. This foundation consists of a capacity to be accepting, open and curious, steadfast, and present. In Part 3, you'll learn exactly how to establish this kind of inner holding environment that will empower you to dissolve the different components of the Anxious Personality.

- Direct Inquiry is the most effective tool to understand and dissolve each component of the Anxious Personality. For the rest of the chapters in Part 2, you'll learn exactly how to do this, and in Part 3, you'll get hands-on experience with the Direct Inquiry prompts and exercises I've provided.

CHAPTER 6

THE INNER CRITIC

T he Inner Critic is the part of our psyche that tries to keep us safe, so its intentions are good. But often, its good intentions are mixed in with harsh judgments. You might be surprised to discover that the Inner Critic is a major source of your anxiety. If the Anxious Personality is like a prison, the Inner Critic is the prison guard. It's trying to keep you safe, but it's doing so while robbing you of your freedom.

The Inner Critic isn't limited to just criticism. It can push, drive you, tell you what's right or wrong, tell you how you should or shouldn't behave, tell you which emotions are okay or not okay to feel, and most of all, it reinforces who you have taken yourself to be. When the voice in your head is criticizing you, that's the Inner Critic. But where does it actually come from? **The Inner Critic is the amalgamation of all the messaging that you've heard from others—your parents, other family members,**

teachers, society and culture. In other words, it's all the stuff you've internalized.

Many people I've worked with over the years have an extremely aggressive and demeaning Inner Critic, and unfortunately, a lot of times they don't even recognize that there's even criticism from the Inner Critic going on. But more importantly, they don't realize that their anxiety is the result of the Inner Critic attacking them. Just imagine that you have someone in your life constantly hanging over your shoulder, whispering to you that, *You're no good. Oh, watch out for that person over there, they might hurt you. You need to do that better! Don't be too pushy, people don't like that. Don't be a pushover, people don't like that.* You can try to ignore it, but it will still get under your skin, won't it? And if you aren't able to back this person off, you'd likely get nervous about things or start getting aggravated. That's exactly what's happening with the Inner Critic in the Anxious Personality.

WHY WE BELIEVE THE INNER CRITIC

The Inner Critic initially is a developmental structure in our psyche to help us appropriately engage in the world. Generally, the Inner Critic develops around the age of seven or eight as we are beginning to separate from our families and become individuals. As an interim "program," the Inner Critic forms as an internalized set of rules to help us know what's appropriate. At the time, we hadn't developed a natural conscience yet, so the Inner Critic is a stand-in for what is right and wrong. Generally, these are messages that come from our parents, primary caretakers, and early environment. All those messages get internalized into an Inner Critic "voice" that heavily shapes our experience.

The #1 misunderstanding in working with the Inner Critic as an adult is we think those messages are true and that they come from us, even if objectively those messages are untrue and they in fact came from outside of us instead of our own inner knowing. Because our parents were by no means perfect, what they deemed appropriate versus inappropriate might have been heavily skewed. So we end up believing that we should be skinnier, or we end up believing that we're not smart enough, or we end up believing that we're selfish people.

So, now that we are adults, we still carry around the interim programming of the Inner Critic. We end up living our life unconsciously believing that we are still dependent on the rules our parents set for us. We don't challenge whether or not these rules are in fact true because we simply had to take it as truth when we were kids. Now, we can challenge any of these messages and find out the truth about ourselves. This can be trickier than it sounds because for most of us, we've suppressed the messages of the Inner Critic so we're not conscious that they are even going on. All we're aware of is that we somehow feel anxious, or sad, or depressed and don't really know why. But it's likely because the Inner Critic just walloped you with a massive judgment.

The problem with the Inner Critic is that it contains old programming that isn't relevant anymore to your life as an adult. For people who struggle with anxiety, the Inner Critic played a major part in keeping us safe by telling us how to be hyper-vigilant:

- *Mom is in a bad mood, so tread carefully.*

- *Dad is being quiet again, so try not to be too loud.*

- *You need to pick up your clothes off the ground or Mom will yell at you.*

- *Don't relax too much, Dad will think you're lazy.*

The Inner Critic helped us to be hyper-alert and aware of our surroundings and people in it, but this alertness often turns into anxiety, where we are constantly aware of potential "threats" and therefore unable to simply relax into being where we are. If we haven't examined this "old code" and how it helped us, we will miss out on understanding why the Inner Critic is here in the first place and why it creates anxiety in us. As we see this dynamic more clearly, we might experience self-compassion and even gratitude–which will actually help us let go of the Inner Critic's old programming.

It's tempting for us to make the Inner Critic bad. As we learn about the source of our anxiety, we naturally want to try to get rid of it. But it's helpful to understand that the Inner Critic in fact is a natural part of our development. It was our very first "operating system" that contained programming to support us, and in many ways, it supported us in developing enough security to grow into a functioning individual. So to effectively disengage from the Inner Critic, we also need to understand the roles the Inner Critic might have played in our history and realize that we no longer need its programming.

IDENTIFYING INNER CRITIC JUDGMENTS WITH THE INNER CRITIC INVENTORY

The first step to dismantling the Inner Critic is to use Direct Inquiry to see what specific judgments the Inner Critic says to you through multiple repeating question exercises. This is going to help you see the Inner Critic more clearly, but also see how much it's taking up your mental space. You'd be surprised how much it helps simply to be aware of these judgments, so try to keep an open mind as you're going through this exercise.

Earlier, you learned that the Inner Critic is the part of the psyche that has internalized judgments and "shoulds" about how you should look, how you should be, how you should feel, etc. To organize our insights, I use the Inner Critic Inventory, which categorizes the dimensions of the Inner Critic that are most important to creating the Anxious Personality. **You'll be able to complete this inventory in the workbook portion of Part 3.** For now, here's a quick summary of the dimensions:

1. **The Mattering Dimension:** How does the Inner Critic keep you from feeling like you matter or that it's okay for you to take up space?

2. **The Value Dimension:** How does the Inner Critic push you to be "perfect" in some way or keep you from relaxing without striving?

3. **The Autonomy Dimension:** How does the Inner Critic tell you to prioritize others over yourself, and whether it's okay to stand on your own.

4. **The Power Dimension:** How does the Inner Critic tell you that power, strength, or anger is not okay?

5. **The Trust Dimension:** How does the Inner Critic judge you when you don't know how to proceed or are uncertain about something?

6. **The Compassion Dimension:** How does the Inner Critic judge sadness, vulnerability, or tenderness?

7. **The Body Image Dimension:** How does the Inner Critic judge your body and the way you move through your life?

As you explore your Inner Critic judgments, you'll start to see the ways in which the Inner Critic keeps you from fully accessing these dimensions in your life. For example, if the Inner Critic is constantly judging anger and keeping you from feeling it, it's also keeping you from accessing your natural, inherent power. Or if the Inner Critic continually pushes you to be perfecting or achieving all the time, it's also keeping you from realizing your intrinsic self-worth. As long as we're disconnected from these different dimensions and natural qualities in us, we'll experience some sense of underlying anxiety. But as we disengage from the Inner Critic, we naturally reconnect with these qualities, which we need in order to truly free of anxiety.

THE DISARMING TECHNIQUE

Hopefully, you're starting to see more clearly the dynamic of the Inner Critic and how it operates in you. In this stage of the Inner Critic process, you'll learn how to disarm and disengage from the Inner Critic. Before we do this, it's worth calling out a few things that don't work:

- Trying to prove the Inner Critic wrong
- Ignoring the Inner Critic
- Trying to overpower the Inner Critic

All of these tactics give the Inner Critic more power and reinforce the dynamic. In a way, it's like quicksand. The more you fight, the more caught up in the Inner Critic's judgments you get. Instead, the primary technique to disarm the Inner Critic is through understanding and awareness. That's easier said than done, and disarming the Inner Critic is a skill that you build and get better at. But when you master this technique, the "gatekeeper" of the Anxious Personality goes on hiatus.

As we've mentioned before, the Inner Critic has many, many layers to it. But addressing the Inner Critic is like riding a bike. At first, it's easy to lose our balance and fall. But we learn how to make micro-adjustments because we get better at noticing when we're about to lose our balance. As you gain more awareness of the Inner Critic, you can start to spot it more easily.

The purpose of disarming the Inner Critic is to experientially dis-identify with how the Inner Critic has impacted us and to realize the truth of who we are. Notice that I'm saying that we need to "experientially dis-identify" with our self-image. It's important for us not to simply recognize an Inner Critic attack and mentally say to ourselves, "Well, that's just an Inner Critic attack and I'm going to dis-identify with this feeling of being small and powerless." In order for us to really be free of the Inner Critic dynamic, we need to experience it somatically in our bodies and feel exactly how the Inner Critic has impacted us, how it has made us feel, and how we've come to identify with its judgments and simply believe them to be true.

So how do you disarm the Inner Critic? The most effective way that I've come to learn how to disarm the Inner Critic is with the following steps:

Step 1: Identify the Specific Inner Critic Message

What you've done so far is to begin gaining more awareness of the Inner Critic messages that occur in the Anxious

Personality. But I can't emphasize enough how important it is to **get clear on the specific words the Inner Critic is using.** Why? Because sometimes we can have a vague sense of the Inner Critic attacking us, but without knowing *exactly* what it's saying, the Inner Critic still remains under the surface of our awareness. When it's there, it's difficult to create enough psychological distance from it to disarm it.

This first step is critical to effectively dealing with the Inner Critic and **cannot be skipped,** even though you'll be tempted to do that. What I often ask my clients when they are stuck in an Inner Critic judgment is, "What are the specific words the Inner Critic is using?" If they don't have clarity on that yet, the rest of the steps become less effective.

Step 2: Externalize the Inner Critic

One of the key ways for us to separate from the Inner Critic and stop believing its messages is for us to externalize it. When we do this, we're able to see the Inner Critic dynamic more clearly and experientially understand its impact on us.

Close your eyes and visualize the Inner Critic outside of yourself. To get a better sense of the Inner Critic, ask yourself these questions:

Size and Shape:
- Is the Inner Critic big and solid?
- Is it bigger than you or smaller than you?
- Is it all around you, like a cloud or fog?
- Is it heavy? Or is it light?

- Does it have a texture to it? Is it like iron or brick? Or is it spongy?

Orientation & Position:
- Is the Inner Critic in front of you or behind you? Or is it all around you?
- Is it looming above you? Is it facing you?

Personal History:
- Can you tell if the Inner Critic is a person in your history? Like a mother or father, or an older sibling? Or a teacher?
- Or is the Inner Critic a combination of multiple people in your personal history?
- Is the Inner Critic message cultural or societal? When and how did you get this message?

Attitude:
- What kind of attitude does the Inner Critic have toward you?
- Is it arrogant and disdainful?
- Is it more like a coach, wanting to motivate you?
- Is it well-intentioned or simply mean?

After you've done that, notice what it's like to have externalized the Inner Critic. Do you feel like there is more distance between you and the Inner Critic? Is it easier to accept that when you are criticizing yourself, it's actually the Inner Critic and not you? Why do we explore all these different aspects of the Inner Critic? Because the more we're aware of the Inner Critic, the easier it is to disengage from it. We get clearer about exactly what it is, where it came from, and exactly how it shows up in us.

Step 3: See How the Inner Critic Makes You Feel

See how the Inner Critic is making you feel without judging it or avoiding your experience. A lot of times, the Inner Critic will make us feel small, weak, unimportant, not confident, powerless, or simply just bad about ourselves. It's important for us to see this dynamic without trying to immediately get out of it or react to it because it creates an inner space for us to hold our experience. When we can be with our experience without judging it, it shifts us into being ourselves in a different way—not small and powerless, but compassionate and understanding.

See if you can stay with whatever feelings are arising in relationship to the Inner Critic as best you can. Feel its impact on you. If it is making you feel sad and depressed, simply hold that experience with compassion. If it is making you feel angry, then allow that anger to be there. If it is making you feel powerless, what is it like to let yourself feel powerless? Stay with whatever experience you are having for a few minutes. Being with the impact of the Inner Critic is like a muscle we build so we can disengage from its criticisms. So remember to breathe and sense yourself as fully as you can without judging the experience or trying to get out of it.

At this point, you might experientially feel like a child again or it might bring up painful memories of the past. As best you can, simply be with that experience, feeling the impact and at the same time witnessing the experience as you are now. As you're holding this experience, see what naturally wants to arise. Is there anger present? Or compassion? Or maybe a sense of love? See if you can let what naturally wants to come forth actually be present with you now.

Notice what happens if you let your body completely express what it wants. So if there is anger, what is it like to let yourself clench your fists or hit a pillow? If there's compassion, what is it like to give yourself a gentle hug? If it is love, what is it like to put your hand on your heart? Give yourself what you naturally would give to a small child if someone had criticized them and see what happens.

Step 4: Disarm the Inner Critic

Option 1: Shrink the Inner Critic

Visualize the externalized Inner Critic figure shrinking to a miniature, action-figure sized entity. You might imagine its voice getting higher and less powerful. Or maybe it loses its voice altogether. As it shrinks, see what it's like in relationship with you. Does it lose some of its power? Do you feel larger and more substantial? Notice how you feel with the Inner Critic super tiny. What is it like to have more inner space? Does it feel strange and unfamiliar? Does it feel good? If you'd like, feel free to squish the Inner Critic between your finger and thumb, just for fun and see what happens. What's it like to have squished it? How do you see yourself now?

Option 2: *Riddikulus*!

In the Harry Potter series, *Riddikulus* is a charm that is used in defense against a Boggart, which is "a shape-shifting creature that will assume the form of whatever most frightens the person who encounters it." What's interesting about the Boggart is that "it is not and never has been truly alive." So it is much like the Inner Critic in that way. The students of Hogwarts learn the *Riddikulus* charm, which causes the Boggart to assume a form that is humorous to the caster and dispels the Boggart's ability to terrorize. Boggarts are defeated by laughter, so forcing them to assume an amusing form is the first step to defeating them.

The Inner Critic is a lot like Boggarts, and we can sometimes perceive them with fear and trepidation. As a result, we give its voice a lot of power when it deserves no power at all. In this defense technique, practice making the Inner Critic ridiculous in whatever way you wish and see if humor can help you disengage from the Inner Critic's message. You might imagine it choking on its words. You might, like Neville Longbottom in the books, put the Inner Critic in funny clothes. See what makes you laugh, and then notice how you feel in your body in relationship to the "ridiculous" Inner Critic. When you feel good about it, feel free to make the Inner Critic disappear in the most comedic way you can think of.

Option 3: Befriend the Inner Critic

Remember that the Inner Critic was an integral part of your development and helped you survive. In this technique, see what the Inner Critic is trying to do to protect you. It might be trying to get you approval so you can succeed. It might be trying to get you to hide so you won't run the risk of being criticized or humiliated. It might be pushing or driving you to do something "better."

Most of what the Inner Critic is trying to do is based on instinct and survival, so once you get in touch with what it is saying, feel into what it is really needing. What's it wanting to provide you? Usually, these are very essential qualities that every child needs that might have been missing from the environment, so the Inner Critic had to step in to make sure you could survive. In feeling compassion for the Inner Critic's misguided efforts to protect you as a child, you reclaim your own power. Common needs that the Inner Critic is trying to get for you are:

- Love
- Support
- Value
- Compassion
- Understanding
- Space
- Strength
- Willpower
- Peace
- Acceptance
- Safety

When you identify one of these needs, what happens when you simply accept that the Inner Critic is trying to make sure you get the need met? What happens when you sense into the need itself? Now turn toward yourself—what is it that you're needing that you're actually not receiving from the Inner Critic? How does it feel to acknowledge that? As you sense what you're needing, can you allow that to arise in your experience?

Step 5: Integrate Your Present Experience

It's important in this final step to connect with the experience of inner spaciousness without the Inner Critic chattering away at you. In this step, you might notice how your experience is different. What is it like to have freed yourself from the Inner Critic, at least temporarily? When you disarm the Inner Critic, you'll be able to more easily access and recognize your true qualities—your inner strength, your authentic capacity, your real goodness, your compassion and love, and most importantly, you'll feel what it's like to be yourself without all that criticism.

NEXT STEPS

This technique takes practice. When I first started disarming the Inner Critic, I felt like Neo in *The Matrix*, finally turning to face these agents that were programmed to keep me trapped. For my entire life, I had either bought into the program or had run from it. But then I realized I *could* be free of it. But like Neo, when I first turned to face the Inner Critic, I got knocked down a lot. I hadn't understood enough of the truth to defeat the programming outright.

But then, after time, I would learn how to see the Inner Critic attacks coming and start to see through its false claims. The judgments started to come in more slowly, and I could see where they came from and how they came from someone else's idea of how I should be instead of my own inner knowing. Finally, like Neo at the end of *The Matrix*, the Inner Critic no longer had power of me, and it was as if I could simply disarm its bullets simply by being myself. At this point, we've mastered the technique because we've reclaimed our inner authority and given ourselves permission to live our own lives.

SELF-REFLECTION

To get a sense of where you might be in the process of freeing yourself from the Inner Critic, consider the following questions:

- Are you aware of the Inner Critic and the specific messages it gives you? Or are you identified with the Inner Critic and believe yourself to be the one criticizing yourself.

- Do you have a way of disengaging from the Inner Critic that isn't ignoring it or fighting it?

- Are you aware of the more subtle ways the Inner Critic impacts how you feel and how you act?

- Do you have a clear understanding of what it's like to be completely free from the Inner Critic?

The Inner Critic is a major gateway to freeing yourself from anxiety. Many of my clients work on this component of the Anxious Personality and feel a complete shift in their anxiety. But this also isn't an easy technique to master. If you're feeling overwhelmed by these steps or aren't getting the results you want, don't worry. Remember that we always start with self-acceptance. So take a breath, notice where you are, and connect with your own support and compassion before moving onto the next chapter.

KEY CHAPTER TAKEAWAYS

- The Inner Critic initially is a developmental structure in our psyche to help us appropriately engage in the world. Generally, the Inner Critic develops around the age of seven or eight as we are beginning to separate from our families and individuate.

- The Inner Critic is the amalgamation of all the messaging that you've heard from others—your parents, other family members, teachers, society and culture.

- The #1 misunderstanding in working with the Inner Critic as an adult is we think those messages are true and that they come from us, even if objectively those messages are untrue and they in fact came from outside of us instead of our own inner knowing.

- You can complete the Inner Critic Inventory in Part 3 to bring more awareness to what the Inner Critic says to you, how it impacts you, and where in your history it came from.

- To effectively disengage with the Inner Critic, we need to apply the Disarming Technique to fully disidentify with it and reclaim power and authority over our own lives and actions.

CHAPTER 7

THE SENSE OF SELF

T he Anxious Personality has a particular Sense of Self that is different from other personality types. The Sense of Self is generally defined as a core identity—how you see yourself and how you want others to see you. The Anxious Personality, regardless of the anxiety patterns it expresses, is particularly invested in thinking of itself in a certain way i.e. primarily that it is not confident, deficient somehow, and therefore anxious. At first glance, the Sense of Self isn't really a problem. But with the Anxious Personality, there is anxiety embedded into each of these ways of viewing oneself.

- This anxiety says, "If I am *not* easygoing or if I express what I'm really thinking, then I'll lose connection."

- This anxiety anticipates, "If I exceed expectations and do things perfectly, then I'll be safe."

- This anxiety thinks, "If the people around me depend on me, then they won't hurt me."

The Sense of Self leaves little room for us to see ourselves as we actually are. Instead, the Sense of Self of an Anxious Personality generally believes in an overly deflated view of oneself, which often doesn't match what's actually real.

HOW A SENSE OF SELF IS CONSTRUCTED

Generally, most of us walk around and take for granted that we know what we mean when we use the word, "I." But where does this sense of identity come from? How is it constructed? When did it develop? If we have more understanding around this Sense of Self, we can start to see that we have mistakenly identified with the Anxious Personality.

This is where modern psychology has contributed a great deal to the potential we have for personal transformation. From the now decades of research and practice, we know that **the building blocks for the Sense of Self is something called Self-Images.** The American Psychological Association defines "self-image" as follows:

> *"One's view or concept of oneself. Self-image is a crucial aspect of an individual's personality that can determine the success of relationships and a sense of general well-being. A negative self-image is often a cause of dysfunctions and of self-abusive, self-defeating, or self-destructive behavior."*

Where did these self-images come from? We start developing self-images very early in our childhood development. As we become individuals, we take signals from the environment and our primary caregivers to reflect who we are. This is a process called **mirroring.**

If our environment mirrored our authentic, positive qualities, reflecting back the message that we are strong, loved, capable, etc., we form a self-image that is also strong, loved, and capable. You can see this in young children when they say, "Mommy, look at me!" But if our environment was unable to mirror these qualities, or they reflected a distorted view of who we were, then we can develop self-images that are less positive. We may have had parents who were too busy to see us, so in that lack of mirroring, we got the message, "You're not important." Or if our parents were often frustrated or overwhelmed by us, we may have developed a self-image of "I am a burden." **Anxiety itself is embedded into these self-images.** Here are a few examples to help illustrate how this happens:

- If our environment reflected back to us that we were dumb, we lose touch with our natural intelligence.

- If our environment reflected back to us that we were unimportant, we lose touch with our natural sense of mattering and being important.

- If our environment reflected back to us that we did not belong or something was wrong with us, we lose our natural sense of acceptance and love.

- If our environment reflected back to us that we had to be perfect, then we lose touch with our inner knowing that our value comes from simply being ourselves.

The lack of mirroring leads to an experience of disconnection from what is intrinsic and natural to us. This results in anxiety. Instead of having access to and contact with what is natural in us, we experience disconnection and anxiety. This is why intuitively *we know* that something feels off with anxiety. It is pointing to the fact that this disconnect is real.

THE CORE SENSE OF SELF

There's often a mixture of positive and negative self-images, and even self-images can be conflicting. Through the years, we pick up many self-images, which is why in the case of the Anxious Personality, you can think of yourself as someone who is very competent but also think of yourself as someone who has very little power. Some self-images are conscious and others operate beneath our awareness, which is also why you can feel high anxiety in certain situations even though you rationally see no reason for you to be anxious at all.

Eventually, our minds do an amazing and miraculous thing. The mind takes all of these self-images and amalgamates them into a **Core Sense of Self**, or an individual feeling of identity. It gives you a sense that you are you. This isn't a problem in itself. We absolutely need a Sense of Self or identity to operate in the world. But as we've been exploring, when anxiety is built into the Sense of Self, it makes it more difficult to operate in the world. So we want to be able to understand what self-images contain this kind of "anxiety DNA." As we start to see that we have unconsciously identified with these self-images, they begin to fade, reconnecting us with our own natural and intrinsic qualities that we had previously been disconnected from. These are qualities that are critical for us to smoothly operate in the world—confidence, strength, mattering, value, etc.

THE SENSE OF SELF INVENTORY

To see more clearly what self-images we're identified with, we can use the Direct Inquiry Method to examine our self-images, particularly the ones that have operated in our subconscious. We have a wide variety of self-images, and in general, anything that you can use to "tag" yourself as you can become a self-image. *I am a Democrat. I am a Republican. I am tall. I am fat. I am an intellectual. I am athletic.* The self-images that we are most interested in with the Anxious Personality, though, have to do with the following dimensions:

1. **Love & Acceptance:** We can write many volumes of books about love and acceptance, but I'm referring here to a kind of holding that you received as a child. Did you feel safe and loved? Did you feel

nurtured? Did you feel accepted and that your needs were responded to? If the environment you developed in didn't reflect a kind of safety and security, then as you were forming self-images, you may have taken on a self-image that had a flavor of "I'm not safe."

2. **Value & Self-Worth:** By conventional standards, we think of "value" as what someone has accomplished. Even in our language, we speak about the "net worth" or an individual, referring to how much money someone is worth. What we're trying to understand with this dimension of self-image, however, is an intrinsic kind of worth. Do you feel worthy by just being and not having to do anything? Do you feel valued simply because you are here? Or did the environment reflect back to you that you had to do something to earn your value or worth? Did you have to do things a certain way or meet expectations?

   If so, you may have developed a self-image of "I'm not someone who has value except for what I contribute." This is often a dimension that has conflicting self-images. In my case, I grew up with a conscious self-image of "I am better than most people at many things" and an unconscious self-image of "I am someone who isn't really cared about for just being me."

3. **Power & Confidence:** This dimension of self-image is tremendously important to understanding the Anxious Personality, because it is the dimension that contributes the most to how we operate in the world. Often, people with an Anxious Personality carry around self-images that they are weak, or not confident, or incapable in some way. This is often because the self-images behind this experience are based on the fact that the environment reflected back these falsities. Your parents may have been aggressive or even abusive, which often leads to a self-image of "I am small, weak, and vulnerable." Or if you received a lot of critical messages from your environment, you may have developed a self-image of "I am someone who never does things right." When we carry around these self-images unconsciously, then of course it becomes difficult to operate smoothly in the world, and certainly it becomes nearly impossible to operate with confidence and power.

RECONNECTING WITH THE AUTHENTIC SELF

As I've mentioned in previous chapters, I'm not a proponent of trying to create an "improved" sense of self because these anxious self-images would still be operating in the background. When we don't directly understand these self-images, we miss out on the opportunity to heal and reconnect with the very real qualities in us that never got mirrored—our intrinsic sense of safety and security, love and acceptance, power and confidence, etc. There is healing that occurs when we start to see these self-images, but often seeing them involves re-experiencing some of the hurt and pain of not having been mirrored properly. Feeling the disconnection of having been "missed" requires self-compassion and acceptance. But when we hold this with love, we're able to reconnect with these intrinsic qualities, and the former self-images dissolve.

In Part 3, you'll have a chance to explore getting back into contact with these intrinsic qualities, which I've sometimes referred to as our "anxiety superpowers." Generally, when we have self-images that reinforce our historical disconnection with these qualities, we tend to lose sight of them, so it's helpful to regain our ability to see, feel, and experience them again. When we do, they become like a precious treasure.

Note that we don't need to create new self-images. When we reconnect with who we truly are, we don't need to be anything. We simply *are*. When we're reconnected, the anxiety that resulted from our original disconnection disappears. If we try to create a new self-image but we are still disconnected from our essential qualities, we'll end up feeling fake. For example, if we try to create a self-image of someone who's confident when we're not truly connected with authentic confidence, we'll likely have a kind of bravado that doesn't feel real to us or others. When we do this, we create even more anxiety because we can still feel the disconnect in us and we try even harder to uphold this self-image. And the cycle continues....

NEXT STEPS

The Sense of Self Inventory portion of the workbook in Part 3 uses Direct Inquiry to help you understand what self-images are either conscious or unconscious in each of these dimensions. When you complete them, you can see your self-images more clearly, and how these self-images form a Core Sense of Self. The Direct Inquiry prompts in the same section will help you see how you've identified with this Sense of Self and also *why* you've identified with it. As you gain more and more awareness of these self-images and their history, the easier it is to reconnect with the essential qualities that ultimately help dissolve anxiety altogether.

SELF-REFLECTION

Consider the following questions to help you gauge your level of awareness of your Sense of Self:

- Do you view yourself and your anxiety as "fixed" instead of dynamic?

- Have you examined the various self-images that have formed your Sense of Self?

- Have you explored how your Sense of Self has been conditioned and where its limitations are?

- Can you distinguish the difference in experience between your conditioned, historical Sense of Self vs. being free from preconceived ideas of who you are?

KEY CHAPTER TAKEAWAYS

- The Sense of Self is generally defined as a core identity—how you see yourself and how you want others to see you.

- The building blocks for the Sense of Self are **Self-Images,** which form through a process called "mirroring." We develop a self-image by internalizing what the environment reflects about us.

- The lack of mirroring leads to an experience of disconnection from what is intrinsic and natural to us. This results in anxiety.

- The mind takes all your self-images and amalgamates them into a **Core Sense of Self**, an individual feeling of identity.

- We can use the Direct Inquiry Method to examine our self-images, particularly the ones that have operated in our subconscious, to bring more awareness to the Core Sense of Self and the anxiety that is embedded into it.

- To effectively heal the lack of mirroring, it's necessary to reclaim the authentic, natural qualities that weren't reflected—love and acceptance, value and self-worth, and power and confidence.

CHAPTER 8

THE CORE BELIEF

T he Core Belief accounts for the particular worldview of The Anxious Personality. If the Anxious Personality were a computer program, the Core Belief is like the actual CPU that powers and enables the program to run. It's the core operating principle of the personality, and in a way, is what makes each personality type unique as it orients and shapes the personality according to its Core Belief. How does this work?

The Core Belief is a reflection of how we were and have been disconnected from our true selves, or, in this case, the intrinsic security, holding, and support that is the very nature of who we are. Consider the experience that a good many of us have had growing up of not feeling supported, met, seen, or held by our environment. Because the environment lacked this sense of holding and didn't adequately reflect that you were safe, secure, valued, etc., we end up feeling estranged from what is most natural to us when we are present to ourselves.

Instead, we unconsciously conclude that something must be wrong with us. Our parents or the environment around us are continually mirroring to us that we are not safe, not good enough, not worthy of support, or not valued somehow. Or, in some cases, the environment is aggressive, critical, harsh, and has a general tone of potential hurt. Either way, it wouldn't be natural to relax in these kinds of environments. We end up feeling detached and removed, or we end up feeling the need to protect ourselves. The resulting "tone" or air that we end up breathing and abiding in is anxiety—the general feeling that something isn't quite right, either about us or about the environment. If we were highly sensitive or if we were abused in some way, we develop a sense of hypervigilance and a heightened habit of looking for potential danger and avoiding it.

The worldview that develops then is one where we don't feel safe or supported and that we lack the power to do anything about it. As this worldview becomes more crystalized, the Core Belief tries to reinforce this worldview with data to prove that the world is, in fact, unsafe. But it also filters out any data that doesn't align with this worldview, even if that data is objectively true. This is why for people with The Anxious Personality, any objective evidence of how safe you are, how good you are, how competent and worthy you are results in a "does not compute" kind of experience. It doesn't conform to the existing worldview, and so the Core Belief unconsciously dismisses it.

The Anxious Personality, because of its worldview, ends up ignoring other possibilities and it certainly ignores the truth that you by nature have inner support, capacity, value, and worth, and that there is plenty of evidence that you are safe in the world. As we've explored in Chapter 3, certain anxiety patterns start to crystallize as the Core Belief informs the worldview of the Anxious Personality. We avoid, or we feel as if we need to be perfect, or we constantly anticipate what other people need or want to make sure that we stay safe by doing what's expected of us.

You can see how we begin to form the Sense of Self from the Core Belief. We are constantly receiving input from the environment, and if anxiety is the result over and over again, we start to form a sense of identity around it i.e. "That's just the way I am." All the reinforcement that we've done over all of our experience convinces us that this is who we are. This starts to become so automatic that we don't tend to question it as adults. We avoid situations without noticing it. We make ourselves small without noticing it. We try to be a certain way without noticing it. We look for potential danger without noticing it.

When we continually believe and reaffirm the Core Belief, we also re-experience that anxiety we felt in those moments when the environment around us failed to adequately support us. But again, this cycle has become so automatic in us that we don't realize what's happening—we just feel as if this is who I am. Anxiety becomes like the air we breathe. It's so familiar and natural to us that we don't think to question it, or even believe that life is possible without it.

As we explored in Chapter 3, the Anxious Personality typically has three different Core Beliefs:

1. *"I don't matter, I am not important, so I might as well be comfortable."*

2. *"I am not intrinsically valuable and worthy."*

3. *"I cannot trust others to be safe."*

It's worth at this point looking at an example of how this plays out in The Anxious Personality. Meet Jane, one of my clients:

- Jane's Core Belief is that she has no intrinsic value or worth because she had very early experiences of her environment criticizing her when she wasn't "working" on something, whether it was helping her mother clean or practicing the piano, etc.

- As a result, her worldview has convinced her that she has to be accomplishing things to have value. She can't simply "be" herself because then she would get harshly criticized.

- This worldview filters out evidence of her inherent value, so her value is always tied to external accomplishments. But because she's disconnected to her self-worth, even when she does a great job at work or receives praise from her coworkers, she doesn't really believe it.

- The worldview also doesn't allow for her to relax and "not do" because otherwise she would re-experience the anxiety of her early environment. She'd have to feel how she wasn't approved of or valued simply by being herself.

- Instead, she unconsciously looks for data in her life to reinforce the Core Belief. So she looks for ways that she messes up or is not good enough, or ways that she is lazy. She might find herself constantly apologizing for little mistakes or pushing herself to do better.

- The more she pushes, the more she objectively accomplishes, but because she is disconnected from her true self-worth, the cycle repeats itself and anxiety continues.

THE CORE BELIEF INVENTORY

Because the Core Belief is operating unconsciously, the way for us to unlock and heal it is to bring its existence into awareness. We can do this with Direct Inquiry in two ways:

1. Seeing when your worldview is trying to reinforce the Core Belief.

2. Exposing the Core Belief to new information and directly challenging your current worldview.

As we become more and more aware of these patterns and are able to challenge the Core Belief of the Anxious Personality, we start to see what's objectively true. **With awareness, we start to slow down the operating system of the Anxious Personality, until with enough awareness we can see the Core Belief clearly and turn off the entire system.** Similar to the Inner Critic Inventory and the Sense of Self Inventory, we can use repeating questions to unearth the Core Belief from our unconscious patterning. You'll find the inventory and its corresponding prompts in Part 3.

Healing the Core Belief

Because the Core Belief was formed due to our early environment not supporting us adequately, it inherently contains a level of pain that's caused from our estrangement from true support, value, and security. This is where having an experienced guide is so helpful. It's not only to help with the process of seeing how the Core Belief has reinforced an old (and now limited) worldview, but also to provide the compassion, support, and mirroring that you didn't previously get.

Often, we touch into a great deal of pain revisiting the Core Belief and the experiences that created it. Unfortunately, we can't simply "think away" the Core Belief. It's only by fully experiencing and seeing the Core Belief and its origins that we're able to let it go. When we do, the worldview lightens up and stops filtering out what's true about you, and you can begin to receive inputs from your inner and outer world that you are in fact safe, supported, competent, valuable, and worthy.

This is an extremely sensitive point in The Anxious Personality Framework, so it's helpful to make sure you're giving yourself the support you need, both internally and externally. Healing is possible, and when you heal and you realize that the Core Belief you've been carrying around is not fundamentally true, you're free to contribute to your life and the people around you with ease and also a good deal more love.

SELF-REFLECTION

To help give you a sense of where you may be in the process of unraveling your Core Belief, consider the following questions:

- Do you have a clear sense and experience of your Core Belief?

- Are you able to see when your Core Belief is operating?

- Have you examined how your Core Belief affects your behavior and relationships? Where is it limiting and how has it helped you?

- Are you able to physically sense the Core Belief and its tension?

- Do you feel as if you can challenge the Core Belief? Or does it feel automatic and undisputable?

KEY CHAPTER TAKEAWAYS

- The Core Belief is the central operating principle of the personality, and in a way, is what makes each personality type unique as it orients and shapes the personality according to its Core Belief.

- The Core Belief is a reflection of how we were and have been disconnected from the natural qualities of our true selves i.e. inner power, security, authenticity, etc.

- The Core Belief forms a worldview that we unconsciously try to support by actively looking for evidence that confirms the worldview. At the same time, we disregard evidence that doesn't fit into our worldview.

- You can use the Direct Inquiry Method to bring more awareness to how you confirm the Core Belief and how you discount data that is counter to the Core Belief. This allows you to start opening to other possibilities outside the Anxious Personality's worldview.

- By nature, working with the Core Belief can be challenging and painful because of the disconnection from our inner sense of support, holding, love, power, and security. This is why we develop a foundation of presence and holding for ourselves, or work with somebody to help hold your experience with compassion and support.

CHAPTER 9

THE ANXIETY TEMPLATE

T he Anxiety Template is the programming that tells the Anxious Personality how to relate to others. It sets the parameters of how you believe you can behave and how you think the other person will behave. As you might have guessed already, anxiety is embedded into the Anxiety Template, and it's programmed in a way that generally disowns your power and gives it to others. This is the primary reason why anxiety is often paired with a sense of helplessness or overwhelm—we're unconsciously giving away the power to deal with things head-on and with confidence. We'll get into how this happens later in this chapter.

This template develops as we form our Core Belief, which subsequently informs our Sense of Self. Because we need a Sense of Self to engage in the world and interact with others, we form a "template" that we unconsciously use over and over again. This concept is based in object-relations theory, which has been well-established by the field of psychanalysis (for those who want to dive deeper into this theory, see the *Fairbairnian theory*). But ultimately, the Anxiety Template comes down to the following:

- **Sense of Self:** We've discussed the Sense of Self in detail in Chapter 7, but how the Sense of Self operates in the Anxiety Template is more specifically about how you actually feel. Your Sense of Self develops into a consistent experience, comprising emotions, thoughts, and behavior patterns. In the case of the Anxious Personality, that experience often includes some combination of fear, smallness, or powerlessness.

- **An "Other":** Because every relationship has two parts, the Anxiety Template needs an "other" to relate to. In most cases, this is whom you were relating to at an early age and contains elements of their attitude toward you (love, patience, irritation, anger, etc.) But the "other" can also include other "objects" that you can relate to, including "the world," God, nature, humanity in general, a pet, etc. We'll go into this in more detail later in the chapter.

  Trauma, to whatever degree it occurred, also factors into the Anxiety Template and how we see the "other." We often suppress our trauma, so when we're thrust into certain situations that unconsciously remind us of our trauma, our psyche and bodies react with fear and uncertainty. As we understand this dynamic, we can more easily stay grounded in the present moment and connected to our adult capacity and confidence.

- **Feeling Tone**: This is the resulting effect of the relationship, which sets the overall tone for how you feel when relating to others. Feeling tones might contain a general sense of sadness, acceptance, warmth, rejection, etc. So it can be positive or negative, but in the case of the Anxious Personality, the predominant feeling tone is generally anxiety.

Like all the other components of the Anxious Personality, the Anxiety Template is largely automatic and we don't realize that it is operating in us and dictating so much of our behavior. But if you take a moment to examine what happens when you are relating to someone and slow that process way down, you'll see that a lot of your behavior is governed by the Anxiety Template. You might see that you unconsciously censor some things you want to say, or you automatically tense up, or you unconsciously contract to become smaller than you are.

A large role that the Inner Critic plays is to ensure that you're following the programming that's coded into the Anxiety Template. It will try to dictate your behavior to stay within the confines of the template, which means that for the Anxious Personality, you are not allowed to confront the other, be bigger than the other, or hold more power than the other. The question we need to ask ourselves is why and how did anxiety get programmed into this template? Why don't other people seem to have this issue? The answer has to do with power and how the Anxious Personality itself relates to power.

POWER AND THE ANXIETY TEMPLATE

Remember the components of the Anxious Personality. It is estranged from the inherent qualities of inner security, support, and value, which forms a Core Belief that in some way convinces you that something is wrong with *you*. This isn't unique to your personality. Everyone with an ego has a Core Belief and an underlying, vague sense that they are somehow flawed. But for the Anxious Personality, there is an added component of safety in which the environment itself has elements of danger or threat. For example, if we expressed big, loud, explosive energy, especially during the toddler years when we haven't mastered self-regulation yet, and if we were somehow put down or punished, the message that being "big" is bad begins to get programmed into the Anxiety Template. In other words, it's not okay to be loud, or in some families and cultures, to be seen or heard at all.

Because we haven't developed the capacity for discernment as children, we rely on our environment to tell us what is okay or not okay, what is safe and not safe. If the environment itself is aggressive or even abusive (physically, verbally, or emotionally), we'll tend to conclude that any sign of power is negative. **We start to see power as dangerous, and this ends up stunting the development**

of our own power. The message "stay safe" gets programmed into the Anxiety Template, and "staying safe" means staying away from power altogether, including in ourselves. We aren't able to discern the different shades of power or realize that it can be used for positive change, to support, or to stand up for others or ourselves. The Anxiety Template can only interpret power as something that will hurt you, and it disregards other possibilities.

This ultimately creates a Sense of Self that is "nice"— someone who gets along with others, is dutiful, doesn't shake things up too much, someone who is dependable, and generally quiet. Safety for this identity means turning inward, because it interprets the external environment as dangerous somehow. **Because the Anxious Personality has disowned its own power, the inner space it turns to for safety also doesn't have power.** This sets up the core Anxiety Template. Your Sense of Self has concluded that it is "nice" and has suppressed your power, so you're nice at the cost of being weak. Meanwhile, the "Other" in the Anxiety Template ends up getting all the power.

PROJECTING THE ANXIETY TEMPLATE

The Anxiety Template explains the common tendency for those who struggle with chronic anxiety to think that power lies outside of them. We see traces of this in the three major Anxiety Patterns we discussed in Chapter 3.

- With the Avoidance Pattern, we avoid situations where our power is called upon.

- With the Perfection Pattern, we are afraid of the power that others have over us, so we try to perfect everything so we are not hurt by that power.

- With the People-Pleasing Pattern, we try to secure alliances with that power by creating a sense of belonging and security, thinking that "you won't hurt me if we are close or you depend on me."

We overlay the Anxiety Template onto nearly every relationship in our lives, although we do this unconsciously before we've learned about the components of the Anxious Personality. Think of your relationships with authority figures in your life and see if this resonates. How have you related to them? How have you felt in these relationships? Was it easy or challenging to feel like you were equals as human beings? Did you still feel that your needs and opinions mattered, or was it more challenging to access them? How did you tend to view these authority figures?

We can illustrate this even more clearly with people we've had no experience with because it's easier to overlay the Anxiety Template onto them. One of the clients I worked with, Jake, was having severe anxiety during his interviews when he'd be asked a question that he hadn't prepared for. He said his brain would freeze up and he'd lose the ability to speak clearly and end up babbling on for a while. We worked on seeing how Jake's Anxiety Template was getting projected onto his interviewer, and he was able to see that he was projecting his mom's incessant criticism about not knowing the answers to things growing up. What was coded into his Anxiety Template was that no matter what he did or how well he did it, there would be some criticism waiting for him.

When Jake saw how he assumed that the interviewer was criticizing him for not knowing, he was able to start challenging that assumption. The Anxiety Template suddenly seemed to disappear, and he could see himself and his interviewers more clearly. He saw how he had the right experience, was well-qualified, and didn't need to know the answer to every question. Jake also saw that his interviewers were usually very kind and supportive, and he eventually went on to secure a job as a designer at a reputable company.

The Anxiety Template is the central reason why the Anxious Personality has so many challenges with other people. Something as small as receiving an email where you can't clearly interpret the person's intent or tone becomes a source of stress. Or phone calls become potential dangers because you can't anticipate what the other person will say and you don't have the extra time to prepare how you'll respond.

DISSOLVING THE ANXIETY TEMPLATE

When we wake up to how prevalent the Anxiety Template is, we can start to recognize it for what it is and more easily reconnect with who we are in the present moment. This takes a fair degree of self-awareness and understanding of all the components in the Anxious Personality, but there are specific ways to accelerate this process. The most effective approach is to integrate your relationship with power and bring it back into balance. We can do this using the Direct Inquiry Method, this time utilizing a kind of Gestalt technique. Gestalt therapy is a well-known approach in psychotherapy and developed by Fritz S. Perls, and generally involves exercises where you are exploring your relationship with some central aspect of yourself or important figure by imagining them in front of you. Here's the primary exercise, but you can find others in Part 3:

Instructions

- **Step 1:** Write a letter to Power as if it is a living being and tell it how you feel about it. This might include your history with expressions of power, whether it was anger or aggression. You might tell it how it hurt you in the past. You might tell it that you're scared of it, that you hate it, that you wish it wasn't around…whatever is true for you.

- **Step 2:** Then have Power write a letter back to you from its perspective. What does it say? How does it feel about you? Try not to edit anything during this step, you might be surprised by what you find out.

- **Step 3:** Often when we do this, we will see that Power is intertwined with some important figure in our lives, like a parent or a teacher. We may have fused them together in our psyche and mistakenly viewed Power as the same thing as that figure. If you have this experience, write a separate letter to that figure and have them write a letter back to you.

- **Step 4:** Repeat the exercise until you feel clear that you are writing to Power in its essential nature, without it being conflated with other people from your life or your past experience.

As you might have guessed, the purpose of this exercise is to sift through our misinterpretation of power because that's the reason why we suppressed it in the first place. When we can integrate power back into our being, our relationships begin to naturally change. The Anxiety Patterns begin to dissolve. You become more present to yourself as you are—a "nice" person but also one who is powerful and confident.

The Sense of Self begins to shift when you integrate this power, because it was historically built on a belief that power is bad and that it's safer not to have it. When we see through the Anxiety Template and realize that power is a natural part of who we are, we become whole. The components of the Anxious Personality no longer make sense, and so it starts to dissolve until all that is left is the real you.

SELF-REFLECTION

Consider this situation to get a better sense of your own Anxiety Template. Imagine "a boss" sitting in front of you. This person has position authority, but other than that, you don't know much about them.

- How do you feel?

- What do you automatically anticipate coming from the other person?

- Does your nervous system automatically withdraw or tighten up?

This might give you a clue into how the Anxiety Template dictates your reactions and behaviors in certain situations, especially when there are power dynamics at play.

KEY CHAPTER TAKEAWAYS

- The Anxiety Template is the programming that tells the Anxious Personality how to relate to others. It comprises the Sense of Self and its Core Belief, our projection onto whatever or whomever we are relating to, and the feeling tone that is created in that dynamic.

- A key step to dissolving the Anxiety Template is to understand the power dynamic that is embedded into it. The Anxious Personality generally defers power to others, which leaves you feeling a sense of deficiency or weakness.

- The Anxiety Template is automatically projected onto the relationships in our life. When we're stuck in a template, we're unable to see ourselves and others clearly and are unconsciously impacted by the anxiety embedded into the template itself.

- Healing and re-integrating our relationship with power makes the Anxiety Template obsolete. When we reclaim and own our power, we're able to engage in a way that's authentic, relaxed, and confident.

PART 3

―――――――

DOING THE INNER WORK

CHAPTER 10

ESTABLISHING AN INNER HOLDING ENVIRONMENT

T he process of dismantling the Anxious Personality is a journey, and in all honesty, it's not for the faint of heart. This is challenging work, but I also believe that it is the most rewarding work you can possibly do. Like any journey, you need to have some idea where you're heading. In Part 2, I laid out our roadmap of the different components of The Anxious Personality, which comprises four major structures in our psyche: The Inner Critic, The Sense of Self, The Core Belief, and the Anxiety Template. I also discussed how to use our compass, the Direct Inquiry Method, to uncover important insights about each of these components and begin to challenge the false assumptions they were built on. When we gain enough understanding and connect with the truth of who we are, the Anxious Personality dissolves.

But as I noted in Chapter 5, Direct Inquiry needs some basic items to make the journey possible. Because this process requires a ton of self-acceptance, we need to make sure there's an adequate inner holding environment to be able to support whatever arises in our experience. The reason for this is because our initial disconnection from our true nature happened because there wasn't adequate support in our external holding environment. As we go back to these areas of disconnection, which is where the source of anxiety happens, we need to provide ourselves with the holding environment we didn't have. I introduced these foundational qualities in Chapter 5, but here's a refresher:

- Acceptance
- Open-Ended Curiosity
- Steadfastness
- Staying Present

These are not always things that come naturally to us and sometimes need to be developed. You might look at this and feel daunted by it, like "Oh crap, I have to do all this work to get to the work!?" The answer is no. You can start your work anywhere at any time, but if you find yourself facing difficulties in the work, you can come back to these foundational elements and ask, "Am I doing this with acceptance?" "Am I actually curious about this, or am I just trying to get rid of it?" "Am I staying with myself?" It's like going on your journey and realizing you're hungry. You just need to get replenished, and these foundational elements will nourish you. Each time you revisit these qualities of presence, it can feel like going to the spa to rejuvenate. Instead of soaking in a hot tub, you soak in self-acceptance and presence. It's good for the soul and for the journey.

That said, there are certain exercises that we can do to help develop these qualities and make them more accessible to us. Just like going to the gym, when we work the specific muscle of self-acceptance or curiosity, it gets stronger. So you can use these exercises to build in the support you need to start and continue the journey of dissolving the Anxious Personality. As a starting point, you can follow the instructions for the primary meditations and exercises I teach my clients below.

Acceptance

As kids, we tend to suppress trauma or emotions that are too difficult to handle, especially if the environment wasn't able to hold them either. So self-acceptance is essential in an inner holding environment as we revisit the components of the Anxious Personality. This is also the #1 skill we need to effectively disarm the Inner Critic, which is the first thing we usually encounter in dissolving the Anxious Personality. Without acceptance of ourselves and even of the Inner Critic, we will tend to fall into the Inner Critic's usual judgments and not effectively see through them. We may give up on the process before we make much progress.

Open-Ended Curiosity

For us to be successful in dissolving the Anxious Personality, a level of sustainable curiosity is required to be present in the inner holding environment. If we aren't curious and open, we likely won't get very far in our journey. Understanding the components of the Anxious Personality is challenging work, but it contains the thrill of self-discovery and a joy in seeing what is true. So open-ended curiosity supports this joy and helps us continue the journey, even if what we come up against is difficult.

How do we develop open-ended curiosity, especially when our culture seems to put so much value on hard work and hustle? How do we allow ourselves to enjoy this process of inner work without being bogged down by all the problems the Anxious Personality seems to create? It helps to recognize what it's like when we see something true during our process of discovery. In other words, we're aligning to the joy of finding things out about ourselves that we haven't known before. Dissolving the Anxious Personality isn't about "doing it" or "getting it done." When we take that attitude, we are likely already identified with the Anxious Personality. Instead, we're just finding things along the way, as if we were going for an adventure and finding different treasure along the way.

Acceptance & Open-Ended Curiosity Meditation

One way to develop these muscles is to practice an open awareness meditation. You can find this guided meditation on theanxiouspersonality.com. For now, here are the steps to the meditation:

1. Close your eyes and let yourself settle into your breath.

2. Take the first couple of minutes to allow yourself to ground, feeling the physical sensations of your body and breath.

3. When you feel grounded, notice what comes up in your awareness, whether they are thoughts, emotions, tensions, etc.

4. You don't have to do anything with them except notice them while staying grounded. You don't have to consciously let them go or change them in any way. You're just noticing what is present.

5. When you find yourself lost in thoughts or emotions, just notice that you've wandered and bring yourself back to noticing what arises in your awareness.

6. If you find yourself judging a certain experience, like pain in your body or an unpleasant emotion, notice that judgment as part of your experience. Again, there's nothing you have to change about it. All you're doing is being with your experience.

This meditation can be done for any duration. Sometimes, it might be helpful to feel as if your body is a container that is holding every experience you have.

Steadfastness

When we are in the process of dismantling the Anxious Personality, we may find ourselves wanting to push through it and fight what we see. When we fight against the components of the Anxious Personality, we tend to lose our ability to see what we need to see about it, or we get overly serious about it and end up identifying with the Anxious Personality even more. Steadfastness simply refers to our ability to stay with our experience and what is true.

That means steadfastness involves a degree of patience—patience with the process, patience with where you are in the process, and patience with what comes up in the process. This isn't about tolerating suffering. This is simply about the ability to be with your process, which leads to a kind of effortless unfolding instead of a stressful pushing that only exacerbates the patterns of the Anxious Personality.

The way we develop steadfastness through meditation is simply by doing it. This sounds simple enough, but it's surprisingly difficult. If you're reading this book, my guess is that you've probably at least tried meditation. But meditation is a lot like going to the gym, so a lot of us start and then drop off. That's okay. Just keep at it, get the Inner Critic off your back, and focus on being with the meditation, whether or not you're filled with distracting thoughts or filled with peace and stillness.

Staying Present

One of the main practices I use to develop this "staying present" muscle is called the Kath meditation. I learned the Kath meditation from The Diamond Approach as it is one of the core practices from their teachings. The Kath is a term taken from central Asian spiritual traditions, but in other traditions it is called the "t'an tien" or the "hara center." The Kath is a point that is the organizing center of our energy. If that feels too New Age for you, just think of it as a grounding center to keep you connected with your physical, present experience.

The Kath meditation is a focused concentration exercise, where you put your attention on the Kath point. This is located approximately three fingers below the navel and three fingers in, depending on the size of your belly. When your attention wanders, you simply bring it back to the Kath point. Focused concentration is a muscle that we don't often train in Western culture, but we need a certain amount of focus to stay present to our experience. This is important because as we dive into understanding the Anxious Personality, we can get lost in all its patterns, thoughts, emotions, and tensions. **We need to be able to stay grounded in our present reality while inquiring into the various components of the Anxious Personality.**

Steadfastness & Staying Present Meditation

These are exercises that you can do at any point during the process of dissolving the Anxious Personality, so don't think that you have to reach a certain "level" of proficiency or development to begin the Anxious Personality Framework. These are qualities that develop simply by doing the work, but these exercises can accelerate or support you in the process.

1. This meditation is usually done sitting in a chair, but however you want to sit is fine as long as your back is relatively straight.

2. Your hands can be folded in your lap as a way to support your focus on the Kath point.

3. Close your eyes and begin by paying attention to your breathing. As you breathe, notice the breath originating from the belly and sense the actual sensation of the belly moving.

4. Like other meditations, if your attention wanders, simply notice it and bring yourself back to sensing the Kath point. If you can't sense any point at all, just focus on the belly in general.

The Amplification Effect

When these qualities work together, you achieve a synergy that accelerates your understanding of the Anxious Personality. It's as if each quality provides a boost to your capacity to recognize and disengage from the Anxious Personality. Suddenly, you are able to see the previously unknown components of the Anxious Personality with more clarity, and contacting areas of disconnection to your authentic nature becomes not only possible, but desired. You can also think of these qualities as dynamic. They show up when it's needed, and when they are developed, they show up effortlessly, making it simple to stay with your experience. They are helpers on the journey, and if you allow them to develop, will guide you to shift from the anxiety of the personality to the peace, security, and expansiveness of your true self. Bolstered by these qualities, you'll be well-supported to complete the Direct Inquiry exercises in the next chapters.

KEY CHAPTER TAKEAWAYS

- Working with the Anxious Personality involves navigating the inner landscape and re-contacting experiences where we have disconnected from our true nature.

- This disconnection often was due to a lack of a holding environment i.e., our caretakers couldn't adequately support or were inadvertently disrupting our sense of being loved and accepted.

- To effectively understand and dissolve the components of the Anxious Personality, it's helpful to re-create the holding environment so that you can support all the emotions, anxiety, or fear that you might encounter.

Chapter 11

DIRECT INQUIRY PROMPTS

W hile we provided necessary context and detail for each of the components of the Anxious Personality in Part 2, you still need a way to do the work to experientially understand what we've talked about. Little transformation will happen if we just understand the concepts without actually experiencing it for ourselves. That would be like looking a route up Mount Everest and saying, "Okay, I understand how to get there, I pretty much know that mountain."

In this chapter, you'll find the Direct Inquiry prompts that are specifically designed to help you gain experiential understanding of each component of the Anxious Personality. Some prompts are for repeating questions, while other prompts are for different kinds of journaling exercises or explorations. As you go through them, you'll start to integrate the insights you gain from these prompts and begin to see how the Anxious Personality operates within you. It helps to keep a dedicated journal for these Direct Inquiry exercises. For your convenience, these worksheets are available to download on https://theanxiouspersonality.com.

COMPLETING THE INNER CRITIC INVENTORY

As we discussed in Chapter 6, we use repeating questions to become more aware of all the different ways the Inner Critic judges who, what, and how we are across several "dimensions." To complete the Inner Critic Inventory, you're going to follow a specific prompt for each dimension of the Anxious Personality's Inner Critic. If you'd like, print out a copy of the worksheets, or if you can use your own journal.

You'll say this prompt to yourself, and then write whatever judgment or message comes up for you. Use the examples provided so you have a sense of common Inner Critic messages that you may have. After you finish the sentence, say "thank you" to yourself, you'll repeat the prompt, and then complete another response. On each page, there is a different prompt to help bring different aspects of the Inner Critic into awareness. Don't worry if you end up repeating judgments, that's part of the exercise. You'll keep doing this for 15 minutes for each dimension. If you have one, use a timer so you know when to start and stop. A few things to keep in mind:

- The Inner Critic loves to jump in on this and judge how you're doing this exercise, so keep an eye out for that. It might even judge you about how many judgments you have, or what kind of judgments you're writing down. Just notice that and you can even write down those judgments as they come up.

- Do your best to complete the exercise in stream-of-consciousness, meaning don't think about it too much. Just write whatever comes up for you. There's no right or wrong answer and no right or wrong way to do this exercise.

- While you're doing the exercise, see what you are feeling in your body. Do you feel heavy, light, constricted, or expansive?

- Are there judgments that feel particularly heavy or impactful? Which ones are easier to brush off and which ones do you believe to be true?

You'll notice that for each dimension, there's usually an emotion associated with it. The Inner Critic often judges these emotions or doesn't allow us to fully feel them, and as a result, it blocks our access to these dimensions. Think of the emotions as gateways into these dimensions. We want to see what Inner Critic messages are constantly keeping us separated from these dimensions.

The Mattering Dimension

Prompt: The Inner Critic tells me I don't matter by _____.

Example: *"...telling me I should never be the center of attention."*

_____

_____

_____

_____

_____

_____

_____

_____

_____

_____

_____

_____

_____

_____

_____

_____

_____

_____

_____

_____

_____

_____

The Value Dimension

Prompt: "he Inner Critic tells me I should better by _____.
Example: "*...telling me that I can't make mistakes.*"

_____

_____

_____

_____

_____

_____

_____

_____

_____

_____

_____

_____

_____

_____

_____

_____

_____

_____

_____

_____

_____

_____

_____

_____

_____

_____

The Autonomy Dimension

Prompt: In relationship to others, the Inner Critic tells me
I should _____.

Example: "*...not upset the other person.*"

_____

_____

_____

_____

_____

_____

_____

_____

_____

_____

_____

_____

_____

_____

_____

_____

_____

_____

_____

_____

_____

_____

_____

_____

_____

_____

The Power Dimension

Prompt: The Inner Critic judges my anger, power, or strength by _____.

Example: *"... telling me that expressing my anger is too messy."*

The Trust Dimension

Prompt: When I am uncertain or don't know something, the Inner Critic says I should _____.

Example: *"...I should figure it out myself and not ask for help."*

_____

_____

_____

_____

_____

_____

_____

_____

_____

_____

_____

_____

_____

_____

_____

_____

_____

_____

_____

_____

_____

_____

_____

The Compassion Dimension

Prompt: The Inner Critic judges my sadness by _____.

Example: *"… saying that I should just suck it up and other people have it much worse."*

_____

_____

_____

_____

_____

_____

_____

_____

_____

_____

_____

_____

_____

_____

_____

_____

_____

_____

_____

_____

_____

_____

The Body Image Dimension

Prompt: The Inner Critic judges my body by _____.
Example: "*...saying I shouldn't be so overweight.*"

_____

_____

_____

_____

_____

_____

_____

_____

_____

_____

_____

_____

_____

_____

_____

_____

_____

_____

_____

_____

_____

_____

_____

_____

Identifying the Inner Critic's Favorite Judgments

If you've completed the exercise above, kudos to you for using the Direct Inquiry Method to gather insights into the Anxious Personality. I invite you to take a breath, sense your body and how it's doing before moving into this exercise. Next, we'll look at the various dimensions you went through to see if there are "themes" to these judgments. It's important for us to see which judgments get repeated over and over again because these are the ones that have generally made the most impact on us and create the scaffolding of the Anxious Personality. Go back through the Inner Critic Inventory and put a star or highlight the judgments that either:

1. Are repeated over and over again.
2. Have the most impact on you.

These are the Inner Critic's favorite attacks that we have internalized the most, so when we become aware of them and address them, we'll feel the most freed up. On the flip side, these are also the ones that have worked for the Inner Critic, which means that they are also the ones that we've bought into the most and have the hardest time disengaging from. But having a basic understanding of how the Inner Critic likes to attack you will help you disengage from it more easily.

For your convenience, you can use the Inner Critic Matrix on the following page to visualize this exercise. Another option is to purchase access to the interactive workbook online, which takes you through each of the Direct Inquiry prompts and visualizes your scores automatically.

HOW AM I IMPACTED?

INNER CRITIC'S FAVORITE JUDGMENTS

WHAT CONCLUSIONS AM I MAKING ABOUT MYSELF?

HOW IS THE INNER CRITIC TRYING TO HELP?

COMPLETING THE SENSE OF SELF INVENTORY

The Sense of Self Inventory is designed to help us become more conscious of the self-images that we are identified with. From Chapter 7, we learned that these self-images make up our "core" Sense of Self (basically who you identify with as "I") and how these formed based on the mirroring you received from your early environment and family system. The following Direct Inquiry prompts will help you see your core Sense of Self and how much we rely on self-images and others to tell us who we are.

In Exercise A, we'll first do a more general exploration of mirroring and how it shows up for you in your life. When we seek mirroring on the outside, we are often trying to get the kind of mirroring we lacked in our development. This Direct Inquiry prompt will begin our exploration of the general themes that your self-images take on.

In Exercise B, we'll begin to recognize what happens to us when we don't get the mirroring we are seeking from the outside. We may experience shakiness or instability because without constant mirroring, we no longer have anything to tell us who we are. Being able to hold this experience is the key to turning inward and reconnecting with the parts of ourselves that we've disconnected from.

In Exercise C, we'll deep dive specifically into which dimension this disconnection is most prominent. The Direct Inquiry prompts in this section are designed to break down the different self-images that you carry around. Each prompt has a series of follow-up questions that will help provide a full picture of how a particular self-image was formed and why you may be hanging onto it.

Repeat the prompt for each dimension until you have 5-10 self-images per dimension. **This means that you'll repeat the exercise for each dimension 5-10 times.** You can print out additional copies of the prompt or complete the exercise in a journal. After you're done with the prompts, you can complete the Self-Images Inventory by writing in the self-images you identified. This is designed to give you a visual of how these self-images work together to form your Core Sense of Self.

Exercise A: The Need for Mirroring

Prompt: Tell me how you want others to mirror you.

Example: I want them to see me as confident and assertive.

Exercise B: The Lack of Mirroring

Prompt: What happens when you don't get the mirroring you want.

Example: *"I feel as if I'm nothing, that I'm completely irrelevant."*

Exercise C: Love & Acceptance Dimension

How do you get others to mirror you so that you feel loved and accepted?

_____

_____

_____

What happens when others don't mirror you that way?

_____

_____

_____

When has your environment or others around you not made you feel loved and accepted?

_____

_____

_____

How did that experience make you think about yourself and who you are?

_____

_____

_____

What happens if you don't think of yourself that way?

_____

_____

_____

Exercise C: Value & Self-Worth Dimension

How do you get others to mirror you so that you feel valued?

_____

_____

_____

What happens when others don't mirror you that way?

_____

_____

_____

When has your environment or others around you not made you feel valued?

_____

_____

_____

How did that experience make you think about yourself and who you are?

_____

_____

_____

What happens if you don't think of yourself that way?

_____

_____

_____

Exercise C: Power & Confidence Dimension

How do you get others to mirror you so that you feel confident?

_____

_____

_____

What happens when others don't mirror you that way?

_____

_____

_____

When has your environment or others around you not made you feel confident?

_____

_____

_____

How did that experience make you think about yourself and who you are?

_____

_____

_____

What happens if you don't think of yourself that way?

_____

_____

_____

Exercise D: Self-Images Inventory

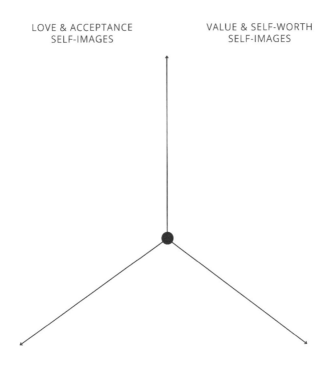

LOVE & ACCEPTANCE
SELF-IMAGES

VALUE & SELF-WORTH
SELF-IMAGES

POWER & CONFIDENCE
SELF-IMAGES

COMPLETING THE CORE BELIEF INVENTORY

As we covered in detail in Chapter 8, we typically gravitate to a core belief that forms our worldview. The Anxious Personality tends to buy into three primary Core Beliefs:

- *I don't matter, I am not important, so I might as well be comfortable.*
- *I am not intrinsically valuable and worthy.*
- *I cannot trust others to be safe.*

We tend to reinforce this worldview by looking for evidence to support our Core Belief, and we also tend to filter out or discount evidence that doesn't match the Core Belief.

We want to disrupt or challenge your assumed worldview by bringing as much awareness as we can to this dynamic. We'll do this by using the Direct Inquiry Method to see more clearly how this is operating in you. These will be repeating questions where you'll respond to different ways you look for evidence to support the Core Belief. In the second part of each prompt, you'll look at ways you disregard experiences that don't support the Core Belief.

Core Belief: "I don't matter."

Prompt #1: Tell me a way you automatically assume that you don't matter.

Example: *"I assume that other people won't really be interested in me."*

_____

_____

_____

_____

_____

_____

_____

_____

_____

_____

_____

_____

_____

_____

_____

_____

_____

_____

_____

_____

_____

_____

Core Belief: "I don't matter."

Prompt #2: Tell me a way you disregard evidence that you matter.

Example: *"When people invite me to things, I don't really believe that they would miss me not being there."*

_____

_____

_____

_____

_____

_____

_____

_____

_____

_____

_____

_____

_____

_____

_____

_____

_____

_____

_____

_____

_____

_____

Core Belief: "I don't have intrinsic value."

Prompt #1: Tell me a way you automatically assume that you don't have value.

Example: *"I assume that others won't like me if I'm not contributing."*

_____

_____

_____

_____

_____

_____

_____

_____

_____

_____

_____

_____

_____

_____

_____

_____

_____

_____

_____

_____

_____

_____

Core Belief: "I don't have intrinsic value."

Prompt #2: Tell me a way you disregard evidence that you have intrinsic value.

Example: *"I don't really believe people when they compliment me."*

_____

_____

_____

_____

_____

_____

_____

_____

_____

_____

_____

_____

_____

_____

_____

_____

_____

_____

_____

_____

_____

Core Belief: "I am not safe."

Prompt #1: Tell me a way you automatically assume that you aren't safe.

Example: *"I assume that others will criticize me."*

_____

Core Belief: "I am not safe."

Prompt #2: Tell me a way you disregard evidence that you are safe.

Example: *"I don't pay as much attention to people around me who are really nice to me."*

_____

_____

_____

_____

_____

_____

_____

_____

_____

_____

_____

_____

_____

_____

_____

_____

_____

_____

_____

_____

_____

_____

_____

_____

Healing the Core Belief

Take some time to reflect on your experience completing these prompts. How do you feel right now? What insights resonated with you the most? As you're seeing how you disregard evidence that challenges the assumption of the Core Belief, how does that shift the way you see yourself and others?

One way for us to heal the Core Belief is coming into direct contact with the truth by opening to it. Before the inner work, the Anxious Personality was like a closed system that didn't allow any new input. See what it's like to open to the possibility that the Core Belief you've bought into might actually not be the fundamental truth. Another way for us to heal the Core Belief is to sit with what we think is the "danger zone" of the core belief. In other words, what's it like to not feel like you matter? What's it like to feel like you don't have value? What's it like to not feel safe and simply be with that fear?

As counterintuitive as it sounds, being with the lack of what we most want and need will bring us closer to it. But when we react, automatically believe it, or avoid it, we don't get that chance. In the following pages, take the time to journal your experiences with these Core Beliefs and where you are in the process.

_____

_____

_____

_____

_____

COMPLETING THE ANXIETY TEMPLATE

The Anxiety Template is where all the components of the Anxious Personality come together and "code" how you engage and relate to others. In other words, it's the core programming of how you move about in the world.

The following exercises deal with two aspects of the Anxiety Template. The first addresses the template itself and clearly understanding how each of the components relate to one another. The second exercise deals with how we project or overlay the Anxiety Template onto situations and people in our lives. When we project onto others, we are letting the Anxiety Template operate how our relationships and interactions will go. Often, this means that we lose contact with ourselves, and we also fail to see the other person clearly or authentically. This disconnection is often another source of anxiety.

The intention for the Anxiety Template exercises is to directly inquire into the **programming of relating**. You'll see how all the insights you've gained into the other components of the Anxious Personality work together to create and maintain anxiety in your system.

Exercise A: Recognizing the Self-Image

Complete the chart based on your insights from previous Direct Inquiry exercises about the Sense of Self and Core Belief. Underneath every interaction with another person, you have the Core Belief that is the driving force behind your worldview. This creates a particular self-image, which has its own feeling and emotional tone. Based on this self-image, we make assumptions about the other person, generally not because of any specific evidence but simply because that is what is coded into the Anxiety Template.

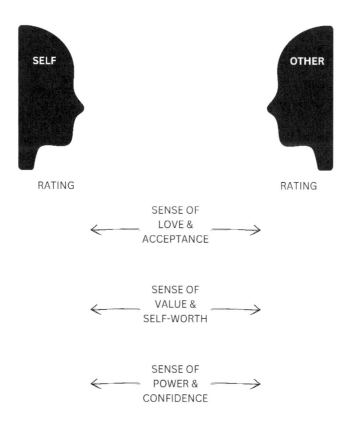

Exercise B: Recognizing Core Relationship Dynamics

The Anxiety Template also takes inputs from the Sense of Self to determine certain dynamics across the three major dimensions of self-images: Love & Acceptance, Value & Self-Worth, and Power & Confidence. Because of the way the Anxious Personality is structured, it views these dimensions as dependent upon another and limited in quantity. While the truth is that there is an infinite, unquantifiable amount of love, value, and power, the Anxiety Template assumes that one person should have "more" or "less."

Take a moment to reflect on your automatic assumptions about yourself and others as they relate to these dimensions. According to your template, do you automatically assume you don't have something that the other person does? In the worksheet, rate how much of each dimension you feel you have vs. the "other."

_____

_____

_____

_____

_____

_____

_____

_____

_____

_____

_____

Exercise C: Recognizing the Inner Critic

Remember that the Inner Critic is programmed to keep the Anxious Personality fixed and static. In the Anxiety Template, it's in charge of making sure your behavior "fits into" the template's programming. It not only wants your behavior to be predictable, it also wants the other person to behave in a particular way to ensure that you get safety, love, mirroring, etc. In this worksheet, fill out the three different prompts to get clarity on how the Inner Critic dictates your relationships. You'll list the Inner Critic message, your subsequent behavior, and how you expect the other person will behave.

INNER CRITIC	YOUR BEHAVIOR	HOW YOU WANT THE OTHER TO RESPOND
_____	_____	_____
_____	_____	_____
_____	_____	_____

Exercise D: Seeing the Anxiety Template

Describe the situation in which you're experiencing anxiety, then complete the chart below.

_____

_____

_____

	SELF	HOW ARE YOU SEEING THE OTHER PERSON?
Self-Image		
Core Belief		
Feelings & Emotions		
Love & Acceptance		
Value & Self-Worth		
Power & Confidence		
Inner Critic		
Behavior		

Seeing the Anxiety Template (Example)

"I had a one-on-one meeting with my manager today. He asked me to lead a new project and I was really feeling anxious about being able to do it. The meeting was fine but I'm not really sure if my manager trusts that I can do it after howI responded."

	SELF	HOW ARE YOU SEEING THE OTHER PERSON?
Image	*"I am not capable."*	*"I'm seeing the other person as not very supportive."*
Core Belief	*"I don't have value and need to prove that I do."*	*"If my manager doesn't think I do a good job, then he'll think I'm not a good employee."*
Feelings & Emotions	*"Anxiety, fear, a sense of overwhelm."*	*"I think he's frustrated and a little annoyed"*
Love & Acceptance	*"I feel like I have to do a good job to be accepted."*	*"I want him to accept me and appreciate me."*
Value & Self-Worth	*"Low sense of self-worth right now, I wish I was better."*	*"I really believe I won't be able to handle his feedback or criticism."*
Power & Confidence	*"I don't feel like I have much power in this situation."*	*"He has all the power. I mean, he's my manager."*
Inner Critic	*"Do a good job, don't make mistakes.*	*"He's going to be disappointed if I don't do a good job."*
Behavior	*Overwork*	*"I want him to praise me and tell me I did a good job."*

Exercise E: Projecting the Anxiety Template

We want to be clear in these situations what is objectively happening versus what unconscious and automatic coding is driving your reaction or response. To do this, we want to examine potential history that might be present and see exactly how the Anxiety Template is getting projected. You can use the example above to see how this projection might happen.

In your journal or on this page, take a moment to explore whether you've had similar experiences before. How old were you? What was the situation like then? How did it impact you, and can you let yourself feel the visceral, physical experience of it? We also want to bring attention to how much we are reading into the other person's words or behavior. Look at your comments in the column, "How are you seeing the other person?" See if these comments are **perceptions vs. objective truth**. Are you sure they aren't being supportive? Are you positive that they will respond negatively? How do you know with 100% certainty that this person is frustrated, angry, or aggressive?

_____

_____

_____

_____

_____

_____

_____

_____

NEXT STEPS

Once you've completed the exercises in this chapter, take some time to reflect on what shifts you might have experienced. What did you see about yourself that resonated? What still feels unclear and murky to you? As you might have guessed, dissolving the components of the Anxious Personality isn't a "one and done" sort of thing. While it may be possible to have an insight and completely be free of all the anxiety embedded in these components, it's more common for it to dissolve a little bit at a time.

Anxiety loses its power each time we disarm the Inner Critic, each time we discover a new self-image we weren't conscious of, each time we notice how we're buying into the Core Belief, and each time we see how we're projecting the Anxiety Template in a relationship. Because of this, I recommend doing the exercises in Chapter 11 multiple times. It will reveal new insights and aspects of the Anxious Personality that you haven't seen before.

I also recommend keeping these exercises in a dedicated space where you'll be able to look over them again. The components of the Anxious Personality can be so automatic and unconscious, that sometimes we have a key insight but then forget about it the very next day! Having your completed exercises accessible helps you see more clearly how these components specifically relate to you.

You can also visit https://theanxiouspersonality.com to find more Direct Inquiry prompts and exercises. If at this point, you're feeling excited about the possibility of dissolving the Anxious Personality, that's great! Keep staying present with your process and journey on! If at this point, you're feeling daunted and overwhelmed, that's also great! Why? Because that is where you are right now and exactly where you're supposed to be.

We work on what is in front of us. When we take this attitude with anxiety, we no longer try to get rid of it. Instead, we're simply being with it to understand it, no matter where we are in the process. When we do this, something miraculous occurs. We reconnect with inner power, love, acceptance, security, and confidence. As you understand each of the components of the Anxious Personality, they will naturally begin to dissolve, setting you free to live a life without anxiety. It's possible, and I wish you compassion, support, and courage on your journey.

CHAPTER 12

CONCLUSION

I invite you to take a breath and notice what it's like to be where you are now. The content, ideas, and techniques in this book aren't simple, and it will likely take some time to digest. That's normal, expected, and absolutely okay. The Anxious Personality might fret that you should be completely healed by now, but that is simply another way the components behind anxiety are trying to maintain their patterns.

If you're feeling overwhelmed, just remember that you can always come back to being where you are. Wherever you are in the moment is exactly where you need to be, and as you create a holding environment for all of your experience, you'll come to know this truth more and more deeply. That said, it's helpful to recap the key points of The Anxious Personality Framework to help you digest and integrate the material.

1. Most approaches to anxiety focus on managing the symptoms and trying to change behavioral patterns. But this doesn't address the root cause of anxiety, which is embedded into the personality structure.

2. The Anxious Personality consists of four major components that create and maintain anxiety.

3. These components are: The Inner Critic, The Sense of Self, The Core Belief, and The Anxiety Template. When you understand how these components work, they begin to dissolve and you're able to reconnect with the authentic source of confidence, value, uniqueness, power, and self-worth.

4. The Inner Critic is the internalization of all the messaging (true or untrue) that you've heard from others—your parents, other family members, teachers, society and culture. It creates anxiety through judgment, criticism, direction, motivation, and constant commentary.

5. The Sense of Self is your core identity, made up of different self-images that were previously formed by how the environment (your parents, family, friends, teachers, culture, etc.) mirrored you. Some of these self-images are painful and untrue, but yet you still believe them to be who you are.

6. The Core Belief is the engine that drives the entire Anxious Personality and forms a particular worldview that inherently creates anxiety. When you unconsciously assume the Core Belief to be 100% true, you automatically look for evidence to support the Core Belief and disregard evidence that contradicts the Core Belief, even if it is objectively true.

7. The Anxiety Template contains the early relational programming of how you interact with others and the world. This template "codes" how all the components work together to create and maintain anxiety in your system.

8. We often project the Anxiety Template onto situations and people in our lives, which perpetuates the Anxious Personality's belief that it is inherently anxious. Recognizing the template when it's operating is the key to dissolving it.

9. Because the components of the Anxious Personality are typically unconscious, you need a way to be able to "see" the underlying system. The Direct Inquiry Method is the key technique to be able to gain the awareness and insights needed to dissolve the components behind anxiety.

10. The Direct Inquiry Method uses targeted repeating question exercises and specific journaling prompts

to "excavate" key insights, experiences, memories, patterns, mistaken conclusions, limiting beliefs, etc.

11. This method doesn't try to bypass any of those experiences by "reprogramming" the subconscious or creating new messaging, since these approaches end up taking us further away from the source of real confidence, authenticity, and self-worth.

12. Healing anxiety occurs when we experientially understand the components of the Anxious Personality and reconnect with the truth of who we are. Understanding these concepts mentally is helpful, but ultimately, we need to be in full contact with our true nature to effectively dissolve anxiety.

If this book has resonated with you, your next step is to begin the work. There are many entry points to the Anxious Personality Framework, depending on where you are on your path to dissolving anxiety. Doing the exercises in this book is a good start. When you do this kind of work, having a guide is greatly supportive. If you'd like help, please feel free to reach out and book a call. If you're not yet ready to receive one-on-one support, there are a variety of other options available to you on at https://theanxiouspersonality.com that will support you in your understanding and development.

Conclusion

I'll conclude with yet another reminder to be where you are, even if that includes struggling with anxiety. As uncomfortable, overwhelming, or scary as it might seem, the anxiety that you've been struggling against for so long is sitting right on top of a priceless treasure. What you've been seeking—self-confidence, self-worth, intrinsic value, inner security, deep acceptance, and inner strength--is right here in this moment. If you can be with the Anxious Personality, hold it, and understand it, its gears will slowly stop churning, its patterns will lose their grip, and the iceberg of anxiety will eventually dissolve.

About the Author

Timothy Lin is the founder of The Anxious Personality Framework. A major component of Timothy Lin's background is deeply integrating various spiritual and psychological modalities. Lin spent 15 years in digital marketing, working with brands such as Toyota Motors, American Family Insurance, and United Health Group. Simultaneously, he served as an ordained priest within a Christian mystic community, facilitated workshops in Nonviolent Communication, and led the Search Inside Yourself emotional intelligence program that was born at Google at companies such as Kaiser Permanente, LinkedIn, and Pulte Group. He has been a student of the Diamond Approach for ten years. He currently lives in Carmel Valley, CA with his wife and two children.

Additional Resources

Visit https://theanxiouspersonality.com for additional offerings to dissolve the Anxious Personality, including:

- **Your Anxiety Superpower Assessment:** Take the 30-question assessment to find out which of the 3 Anxiety Patterns impacts you the most, so that you can take specific actions to understand and dismantle the components behind them. When your anxiety dissolves, you'll reconnect with a specific "anxiety superpower," which is an essential quality that you'll have a unique connection with i.e. compassion, courage, confidence, etc. Receive personalized results instantly with a comprehensive, 40-page PDF report via email.

- **The Foundations of Self-Acceptance: Creating the Inner Holding Environment Digital Course:** Self-acceptance is the #1 foundational element to dissolving anxiety. If we can't accept where we are and we can't accept our anxiety, we'll get stuck in letting the components behind anxiety run the show.

- **Dismantle the Inner Critic in 4 Steps:** Access the full database of Direct Inquiry prompts and complete the worksheets and journaling exercises online. The exercises are interactive and you'll receive instant visualizations and charts to help you